How To Beat Satan at His Own Game

A Guide for Spiritual Warfare

Kathleen Myers

COPYRIGHT

Copyright © 2025 Kathleen Myers

Published by

All rights reserved. No part of this book may be reproduced or transmitted in any form or by any means, electronic or mechanical, including photocopying, recording, or by any information storage and retrieval system, without written permission from the publisher and author.

DEDICATION

To you who suffer, to you who feel alone, to you who live in fear, to you who do not know how to find your way, I dedicate this book to help you move from darkness to light, from fear to bravery, and from war to peace.

To you who put God first in your life, to you who commit your life to Jesus Christ by loving others, and to you who minister to others through your gifts and talents provided by the Holy Spirit, I dedicate this book.

In my own life, I am fortunate to have been married to a man who lived every day serving, loving, helping, and guiding others. He showed them how to receive God's love, to turn to Jesus for compassion and wisdom, and to the Holy Spirit for guidance. Even though Terry is with Jesus, his ministry to others is ongoing. Today, those who lived in despair are not, those who lived in fear are not, those who lived in addiction are not, and those who lived in disbelief are not. In their freedom, others are now free. To his memory of service to his Lord, I dedicate this book.

TABLE OF CONTENTS

INTRODUCTION 6

What Is Deliverance Ministry? 10

Demons 15
    What Are Demons? 15
    How Can Demons Attack You? 17
    What Do You Need to Know About Spiritual Warfare? 22
    What Are Demonic Footholds? 26
    What Are Demonic Strongholds? 29
    What Are Warning Signs of Demonic Intrusion? 31
    How Do You Ward Off Personal Demonic Attack? 36
    What Makes Demons Leave? 41
    What Is The Christian Response to The Demonic? 44

Bible, Prayers, and Spiritual Warfare 46
    What Does the Bible Say About Spiritual Warfare? 46
    What Does Jesus Says About Dealing with Evil? 52
    What Does the Bible Say About the Disciples Casting Out Demons? 54
    What Is the Role of the Holy Spirit in Spiritual Warfare? 58
    What Is Spiritual Warfare Through Prayer and the Bible? 62
    What Is the Armor of God? 66
    What Is the Prayer to Use When Putting on the Armor of God? 70

God and Spiritual Warfare 72
    What Are Some Ways for You to Stay Close to God? 72
    How Do You Rely on God and Not Yourself? 75

How Do We Meet Daily with God Through Prayer and Scripture? 79
What Are Ways You Can Build a Relationship and Hear God's Voice? 82
How Do Demons Respond When You Talk to God? 87

Family and Spiritual Warfare 89
What Is Spiritual Warfare for Your Family? 89
How Can You Pray for Protection Over Yourself and Your Family? 96
How Do I Cleanse My Home and Property of Demonic Influence? 100

Demons and Spiritual Warfare 109
What Are Open Doors? 109
What Are Demons' Legal Rights? 113
What Are Demonic Soul Ties? 118
How and Why Do You Need to Break Soul Ties? 120
What Are Generational Curses? 122
What Is Spiritual Trauma? 124
How Do You Bind Demons? 127

Spiritual Warfare Scriptures 130

EPILOGUE 134

INTRODUCTION

Let me introduce myself to you. I grew up in an affluent, Christian home. I was baptized as a child and was taught about Jesus in the Methodist Church. My childhood was not perfect, as many childhoods are not. My mother had mental health issues. From as early as I can remember, she abused my sisters and me. At that time, I did not know that all of the pain, anger, and disapproval I experienced would have any good purpose in my life. All those terrible experiences taught me how to survive, how to have a passion for Jesus, and how to have compassion for others. I did know somehow I needed to forgive and to not judge anyone. This took years to do. I did not know that everything I went through, God was with me and preparing me for service to others. I just did not understand it then, but I do now.

My life has been centered on God and Jesus for as long as I can remember. However, it did take me a while to fully understand the Holy Spirit. I knew He was there, but did not really understand how the Trinity, God the Father, God the Son, and God the Holy Spirit work together as One. When I understood who God really is to me, I learned God always has a better way and He walks the walk with me daily. That is when everything changed.

In my early twenties, I became a member of the Episcopal Church. In my mid-twenties, I went to work for an Episcopal Church as a lay professional. During this time, I was a Director of Christian Education and Christian Curriculum writer for children and young people, a Christian Education Teacher for Church volunteers, and a member of a multi-denomination Exorcism Team. As God would have it, for about fifteen years He placed me in several different churches as a Christian Education Director, a Church Director of Lay Ministry, a Co-Director and co-author of Lay Ministry School for the Dioceses of Arizona, a Seminarian Christian Education supervisor, a Christian education and goal setting consultant for leadership and teachers in several different denominations around the country, a Pastoral Counselor and an author of Christian Children's books. I had no formal education in Christian Education, Training Teachers to Teach, Pastoral Counseling, Theology, Liturgy, Public Speaking, Goal Setting, writing curriculum and books, and Performing Exorcisms (as it was called in those days). Even though I did not have the degrees, I did have the knowledge and ability to complete these callings from God. What I learned is God walks with you and guides you throughout your life. If you are willing to listen and to follow Him, God will lead you and give you what you need to do His work in the world.

For about twenty years, God sent me to the philanthropic and business world. This provided me with an opportunity to minister to others in a different setting. God had given me ample opportunity to learn about leadership, budgets, goal setting, teaching, counseling, negotiating, raising money, and more. Over the years, I have been the president of a national software corporation, a retail business owner, a cattle rancher, a potbelly pig breeder, an author, and the working president of a philanthropic organization. Amazing, no? There is no way this could have happened without direction from God and His divine intervention.

Today, I am a mother of six, grandmother of ten, great-grandmother of three, and a great-great-grandmother of two. Everything I have ever done in my life prepared me for my next step, even if I did not know what my next step would be. In my early fifties, I became a volunteer in the church. I have been a missionary board member in charge of the missionary houses, a Life Group Leader, an usher, and a coordinator for several Church teaching events. Currently, I am a Life Group Leader, a Prophet Prayer Team Coach, a Sunday morning Intercessor, a Mentor for young women, and most importantly to me, a Deliverance Minister. I can now add to this list that I am the author of a book that can help you enter spiritual warfare with confidence, knowledge, and skill.

I have learned from all of this that in living anything is possible. If you have faith in God and get out of His way, He will lead you, and miracles happen. Things you thought were never possible are possible, and skills you thought you never had become real. So, here I sit as a sample of what God can do if you just let Him. My favorite Bible verse is *Matthew 8:20:* "Fear not, for I am with you always, even unto the end of the age." So, fear not – God is with you, no matter what.

Now back to work:

"How To Beat Satan At His Own Game" is written for people who are interested in more knowledge about the demonic and how demons operate. As well as those who are or may be suffering from demonic attack. Since I am a teacher at heart, it is hard for me not to teach. Therefore, Bible verses are used throughout to verify that the content of this book is biblically based.

The Bible is clear about Satan and his demons being active in this world. The following are a few of the approximately 21 verses in the New Testament that directly mention demons. There are also approximately 49 other verses and 56 mentions of Satan and his demons.

Ephesians 6:11-13

"Put on the full armor of God, so that you can take your stand against the devil's schemes. For our struggle is not against flesh and blood, but against the rulers, against the authorities, against the powers of this dark world and against the spiritual forces of evil in the heavenly realms. Therefore, put on the full armor of God, so that when the day of evil comes, you may be able to stand your ground, and after you have done everything, to stand."

James 4:7

"Submit yourselves, then, to God. Resist the devil, and he will flee from you."

1 Peter 5:8-9

Be alert and of sober mind. Your enemy the devil prowls around like a roaring lion looking for someone to devour. Resist him, standing firm in the faith, because you know that the family of believers throughout the world is undergoing the same kind of sufferings.

Romans 8:37-39

"No, in all these things we are more than conquerors through him who loved us. For I am convinced that neither death nor life, neither angels nor demons, neither the present nor the future, nor any powers, neither height nor depth, nor anything else in all creation, will be able to separate us from the love of God that is in Christ Jesus our Lord."

Jesus gave us authority, as His disciples, to conquer Satan and to help those who are in demonic bondage. We, as believers in Christ and servants to His people, and through the love of God, the powerful name of Jesus Christ, and the wisdom and guidance of the Holy Spirit, can defeat Satan and his demons. God is on our side.

Read, study, and prepare yourself. Then turn to Him for direction. In His infinite wisdom and great love for us, God has given us all of the tools we need to take on Satan's demons and win the battles. Through the power in the name of Jesus Christ and the wisdom and guidance of the Holy Spirit, we can fight these battles without fear. This book is written for the purpose of teaching you and your family how to enter into spiritual warfare and beat Satan and his demons at their own game. It can mean freedom for those you help to become who God means for them to be. All they have to do is say "Yes" to Jesus – they just have to want it.

I will be praying for you as you move forward in your walk with God. May He direct and protect you and those you love. Remember: "Fear not for I am with you even until the end of the age." Amen.

What Is Deliverance Ministry?

The Bible emphasizes God's role as a deliverer, offering freedom from bondage and oppression — both physical and spiritual — through faith in Jesus Christ. While not called "deliverance ministry," the Bible demonstrates Jesus's power to cast out demons and break spiritual strongholds, heal the sick, and comfort the people, which brings healing. This is a core belief of this ministry.

God rescues you from various forms of oppression and bondage, such as demons and Spiritual Strongholds, which hinder spiritual growth and obedience to God. One way this is done is through Deliverance Ministry and the power of Jesus Christ, spiritual healing is available to each of you, as shown in Jesus's ministry and throughout the ages. Jesus, through His teachings and actions, emphasizes deliverance from sin, spiritual bondage, physical afflictions, and the power of darkness. Deliverance offers you freedom and healing through faith in Jesus Christ and the Power of the Holy Spirit.

Jesus As The Deliverer

Jesus' Ministry

Jesus' ministry includes healing the sick and casting out demons, demonstrating His authority over evil spirits, and His ability to deliver you from bondage.

Authority in Jesus' Name

The New Testament emphasizes the authority given to you in Jesus' name, including the power to cast out demons and to heal.

Deliverance as a Spiritual Concept

Deliverance ministry focuses on spiritual freedom from sin and restoration of your relationship with God, along with physical, mental, and emotional healing through the power of Jesus Christ.

Distinction from Exorcism

Exorcism mostly focuses on demonic possession and is designed for unbelievers. Deliverance ministry focuses mainly on demonic oppression and is designed for baptized Christians. Both Exorcism and Deliverance Ministry are designed to cast out demons by the power of Jesus Christ.

Biblical Basis

The Bible provides examples and principles that support the concept of Deliverance Ministry, such as the power of prayer, the power and authority of Jesus' name, and the role of the Holy Spirit.

Jesus' Deliverance from Sin and Bondage

Jesus came to preach the Gospel, the Good News of the Kingdom of God, to perform miracles, such as healing the sick and brokenhearted, raising the dead, and setting the captives of Satan free. Highlighting His role as the Deliverer, Jesus came to offer Himself as a sacrifice for the sins of humanity, so that you can achieve salvation.

Power of the Holy Spirit

Jesus empowers you to cast out demons and to overcome negative influences through the power of the Holy Spirit.

Repentance and Alignment with God

Jesus consistently invites you to repentance as the path to true freedom, emphasizing that deliverance requires you to turn away from sin and align with God's will.

Faith in Jesus Christ

Jesus emphasizes that through faith in Him, you can experience deliverance and walk in the freedom that only God can provide.

Signs of Belief

Jesus states that those who believe in Him will experience signs such as casting out demons, speaking in tongues, and laying hands on the sick for healing. Also, receiving spiritual gifts, which are blessings or abilities given by God to equip you to serve others.

Resisting the Devil

Jesus' teachings encourage you to resist the devil and submit to God, reminding you that through your faith in Jesus and reliance on God's word, you can experience deliverance.

Jesus as the Ultimate Deliverer

Jesus is the ultimate deliverer who sets you free from sin, bondage, and spiritual oppression.

Freedom in Christ

Jesus's sacrifice on the cross is seen as the ultimate act of deliverance, freeing you from the penalty of sin and the power of darkness.

Deliverance from Eternal Punishment

Jesus has rescued you from the "wrath to come" and offers eternal life to those who believe in Him.

Deliverance Ministries are here to help you receive the life God intends for you. So, be eager for deliverance and believe in the delivering power of Jesus Christ.

Deliverance Ministry allows you the opportunity to be set free from demonic influence, through the Name of Jesus Christ and with the help of the Holy Spirit, who was received at Baptism. Deliverance Ministry is designed to cast out demons (evil spirits), which allows you to overcome negative behaviors, feelings, emotions, and experiences. As you become closer to God, Deliverance Ministry also helps to bring freedom to your life and to minister to others in a better way.

Deliverance Ministry believes that as a baptized Christian and believer in Christ, you cannot be possessed by demons, but can be oppressed by them. This means you can be influenced and persuaded by demons to move away from God. Through your sins, demons can oppress your life in ways that affect you mentally, physically, and emotionally. However, you have the help and guidance of the Holy Spirit, living within you. Through the guidance and support of the Holy Spirit, you can receive freedom through Deliverance. By the power of Jesus Christ you will be delivered from demonic attack. The Holy Spirit will continue to guide and support you in your faith journey with Jesus, your Lord and Savior.

Non-Christians, who have not been baptized and have not accepted Jesus as their Lord and Savior, can be possessed by demons. This means that demons can take over your life physically, emotionally, mentally, and spiritually. It is believed that an unbeliever and/or an unbaptized person can be possessed by demons. Unbelievers do not have the same help from the Holy Spirit as baptized Christians do. Since they have not accepted Jesus as their Lord and Savior and/or have not been baptized, a non-believer or an unbaptized person can find it much harder to achieve a good result at Deliverance.

Also, Deliverance can help you by means of your expressions of faith, repentance, and forgiveness. It will aid you in breaking generational curses, soul ties, demonic influences, and more. Deliverance provides you with ways to repent for your sins and to seek and receive forgiveness from God. It also provides you the opportunity for Christ to heal you spiritually and emotionally. Deliverance gives you the opportunity for a new relationship with God, family, and friends.

Note:

Unfortunately, not all Deliverance Ministries are the same. Some are untrained, some are only interested in the money they charge, some really do not have your best interest at heart, and some just make it up as they go along. While others are truly servants of God. They are only interested in doing His will, following methods and practices that have been utilized over the centuries of the Church. God the Father, Jesus, and the Holy Spirit are the heart of their ministry. They depend on the Bible for guidance. Helping people like you find freedom is their highest priority. When you choose a Deliverance Ministry, it is wise to get counsel from others or your Pastor, who has experience with that ministry.

Deliverance Ministry is different from Healing Ministry. Healing Ministry primarily refers to the restoration of your physical, emotional, and spiritual body through prayer and intercession. Deliverance Ministry refers to the casting out of demons in the Name of Jesus. Through the power of Jesus Christ and the help of the Holy Spirit, Deliverance Ministry can help free people from torment, bondage, and oppression, as God the Father continues His steadfast love and protection for you. Deliverance is not a power encounter; it is a faith and love encounter. Jesus's love is extended to you, and your love and worship given to Him.

Demons

What Are Demons?

Demons, like angels, are spiritual beings and do not have physical bodies. They do not live, grow old, and die like human beings, but exist in a spiritual state. Because of this, they have significant power and influence in the world. Although not nearly to the extent of the almighty Creator God, who rules over them, and at Jesus's name that makes them tremble.

Demons are fallen angels, evil, and in the service of Satan. (Lucifer, the leader of all demons, is called different names such as the Devil and Satan. For this book, we will call him Satan). According to the Bible, the very spirit of demons is evil to the core. While we do not know when their rebellion against God occurred, we do know that demons are now completely fallen, desperately evil, and in the service of the supreme ruler of Hell, Satan.

Demons followed Satan in his rejection of God's rule. Demons are under the judgment of God. The Bible confirms that Satan will be chained in the abyss for a thousand years, *Revelation 20:1-3.* In *Romans 10:7,* we find that Christ went to the Abyss. The abyss is described as a prison for demons and Satan, while they await God's final judgment. After the Final Judgement, they will never be free to go out and disturb God's creation. What is written in *Luke 8:31* reflects the picture of *2 Peter 2:4.*

The Purpose of Demons

Demons are bent on killing, stealing, and destroying mankind. They are bent on destruction and stealing souls from God, which causes havoc for mankind. According to *1 Timothy 1-1*, one way is that they seek to destroy by deception. They lead you away from the true Gospel of Jesus Christ and God's purpose in your life. Before the final judgment, they want to destroy as many people as they can, while they have significant power and spiritual influence, they tremble at the name of Jesus, the power of God, and the guidance and comfort of the Holy Spirit.

Satan and all the demons under him are dedicated to following Satan's mission, to steal souls from God, by opposing God's kingdom, by seeking to corrupt humanity, and by destroying as much of God's creation as possible. As a believer in Jesus, who is Baptized in His name, you can be confident and secure in the power of Jesus Christ and in the presence of the Holy Spirit within you; you cannot be possessed, but you can be oppressed, negatively influenced by Demons.

According to the Bible, our goal is to think correctly about these evil spiritual beings—especially their ultimate fear is the name of Jesus Christ.

James 2:19 says that the demons accurately discern God's identity and power. They "shudder" or "tremble" at the thought of Jesus. They are servants of Satan whose only purpose is to oppose God. They will be judged by Jesus Christ.

John 5:2, Jesus is the ultimate judge of all things, including demons. His authority comes from God.

How Can Demons Attack You?

As you know, demons attack you to oppose God's purposes and to deceive God's people in any way they can. Demons can attack you through various means, including tempting you to sin, causing physical ailments, and influencing your thoughts, feelings, and behaviors. They seek to destroy your faith, relationships, or overall well-being.

Demons use a variety of tactics to deceive, oppress, and ultimately hinder you from following God. These tactics are used to control and discourage you, turning you away from God.

Deception

Paul warns Timothy about false teachings that are opposed to the Gospel. Paul does not stop at simply identifying these teachings as false, he says that people who believe false things about Jesus are following the "teachings of demons". *1 Timothy 4:1–3*. This makes sense because demons are in the service of Satan, who is the father of lies and the king of deceit.

False Religions

The Bible seems to suggest that demonic influence lies behind false religions, any belief that opposes the Gospel of Jesus Christ, the Son of God.

The first commandment, "You shall have no other gods before Me," *Exodus 20:3-6*. The prohibition against making idols, bowing down to them, or serving them are warnings against false religions. People who question or reject Jesus have not just chosen a different religion. They are deceived by Satan and are unknowingly serving him and his demons. You either believe in Jesus as the Son of God or you believe some form of the teachings of Satan and his demons, which are all lies and deceit.

Possession

Demons can take control of your body, mind, emotions and soul, which is when they exert control over your actions, feelings, and thoughts. While the exact phrases "demonic possession or oppression" or "Deliverance" are not used, the Bible does describe people being "possessed" by demons. In many accounts in the Bible, we see that demons can possess people.

The goal of possession is total destruction of the person being possessed, *Mark 5*. The demons' goal is to steal souls from God. As an example, after Jesus ordered the demons to leave the body of the person, He decided to send the demons into the pigs. The pigs then ran off a cliff and died. Only the power of Jesus could conquer and control the demons trying to steal the man's life and soul. Demons can possess only those who have not been Baptized and do not profess Jesus as their Lord and Savior. Because of this, these people are exposed to the possibility of complete demonic control over their lives.

Oppression

It is important to note that the Bible does not suggest that demons can possess Christians who have faith in Jesus Christ as their Lord and Savior. Those who have been Baptized and have faith in Jesus have the Holy Spirit living within them. "Therefore take up the whole Armor of God, that you may be able to withstand in the evil day, and having done all, to stand firm." *Ephesians 6:13.* Demons cannot coexist with the Holy Spirit. A Christian who has been baptized and is a believer in Jesus, cannot be possessed. A Christian can be influenced to sin and to do evil through demonic attacks in your mind, body, and emotions. This is called demonic oppression.

Manipulation

Demons may subtly guide you towards destructive behaviors and choices, often appealing to your desires and vulnerabilities. This is true for all people. This can involve tempting you with earthly possessions, pleasures, or power. They can blind unbelievers and persuade some Christians to ignore the gospel. They can empower other religions and practices that oppose Christianity.

"And even if our gospel is veiled, it is veiled to those who are perishing. The god of this age has blinded the minds of unbelievers, so that they cannot see the light of the gospel that displays the glory of Christ, who is the image of God." *2 Corinthians 4:3-4.*

Fear and Intimidation

Demons can use fear and intimidation to control and discourage you from seeking God or embracing your faith. This can create a sense of powerlessness or vulnerability.

"God has not given us a spirit of fear but of power, love and of a sound mind." *2 Timothy 1:7.* The total opposite of an intimidated spirit. So, you see, when you are intimidated, it is a scheme of Satan and not of God.

Promoting Evil Destruction

Demons are often associated with causing harm, suffering, and chaos in the world, mentally, emotionally, physically and spiritually. The Bible describes demons as spiritual beings who actively seek to attack and influence the world through possession of Christians. These attacks can take various forms. Such as deception and temptation which causes you to suffer. Demons' goal is to hinder God's purposes and His people. God, in His sovereign plan, has allowed the influence of Satan and his demons to continue in this world until the day of his final judgment by Jesus.

For Christian believers, "Put on the full armor of God, so that you can take your stand against Satan's schemes. For our struggle is not against flesh and blood, but against the rulers, against the authorities, against the powers of this dark world and against the spiritual forces of evil in the heavenly realms." *Ephesians 6:10-12.*

Doubt and Discouragement

Demons can sow seeds of doubt and discouragement, making it harder for you to believe in yourself or your faith. They may try to make you feel unworthy or hopeless. "For I am convinced that neither death nor life, neither angels nor demons, neither the present nor the future, nor any powers, neither height nor depth, nor anything else in all creation, will be able to separate us from the love of God that is in Christ Jesus our Lord." *Romans 8:38-39.*

Pride and Self-Reliance

Demons can encourage pride and self-reliance, leading you to believe you do not need God or His guidance. This can manifest as a resistance to humility and a rejection of God's authority. "A man's pride will bring him low, but a humble spirit will obtain honor." *Proverbs 29:23.*

Division and Hatred

Demons can incite division and animosity within communities, particularly within the church. They can exploit conflicts and misunderstandings to weaken the unity of believers. Be sure and watch out and avoid those who cause divisions and create obstacles contrary to the doctrine that you have been taught. "I urge you, brothers and sisters, to watch out for those who cause divisions and put obstacles in your way that are contrary to the teaching you have learned." *Romans 16:17.*

Attacks on Faith and Hope

Demons will try to erode your faith and hope, making it harder for you to persevere in the face of adversity. They may attack your sense of purpose and meaning in life. "You believe that there is one God; you do well. Even the demons believe and shudder!" *James 2:19.*

Exploitation of Vulnerabilities

Demons often seek to exploit vulnerabilities in your life, such as past hurts, unresolved issues, or unmet needs. This can involve targeting areas where you are most susceptible to their influence. "For certain individuals whose condemnation was written about long ago have secretly slipped in among you. They are ungodly people, who pervert the grace of our God into a license for immorality and deny Jesus Christ our only Sovereign and Lord." *Jude 1:4.*

Use of Temptation

Demons may use various forms of temptation to lure you away from God, such as tempting you with material wealth, pleasures, or power. This can involve appealing to your desires and vulnerabilities. When tempted, you can say, "God is tempting me." God cannot be tempted by evil, nor does He tempt anyone. *James 1:4.*

Encouragement of Idolatry

Demons may encourage idolatry by promoting the worship of false gods or the pursuit of worldly idols. This can involve diverting your attention and allegiance from God to other things. "No, but the sacrifices of pagans are offered to demons, not to God, and I do not want you to be participants with demons. You cannot drink the cup of the Lord and the cup of demons too; you cannot have a part in both the Lord's table and the table of demons." *1 Corinthians 10:20-23.*

Use of False Teachers and Teachings

Demons may utilize false teachers and teachings to deceive you and lead you away from the truth. This can involve spreading misinformation, promoting false doctrines, and twisting God's Word. Scripture states that false doctrines have a demonic origin: "in later times some will depart from the faith, giving heed to deceiving spirits and to doctrines of demons." *1 Timothy 4:1-2.*

What Do You Need to Know About Spiritual Warfare?

You need to understand that spiritual warfare is a concept within Christianity that involves a battle against demons. It is about recognizing the unseen conflict and actively resisting the influence of demons through faith, prayer, and obedience to God.

The Reality of Spiritual Warfare

It Is Not Just a Concept

Spiritual warfare involves recognizing the reality of evil spiritual forces and how they can negatively impact your life.

Demonic Activity Is Real

Scriptures, especially the Gospels, show instances where Jesus encountered and cast out demons, demonstrating their power and influence.

It Is Not Always Dramatic

While some instances might involve dramatic displays, spiritual warfare can also manifest subtly in areas such as your mind, emotions, and body.

Deception Is the Primary Weapon

Demons associated with Satan use deception to mislead and deceive you.

Spiritual Darkness

Demons seek to create darkness, hinder, or end your relationship with God.

Personal Attacks

Demons can target you with lies and temptations.

Jesus Has Authority

Jesus has authority over the spirit world, and believers can draw on that authority.

The Power of God's Word

God's Word, including the Bible, is a powerful weapon against demons.

Prayer Is Essential

Prayer is a way for you to connect with God's power and ask for protection and guidance.

Armor Of God

You can use the Spiritual Armor as a shield of faith. Each piece can help protect you from demonic attack. The Sword of Righteousness, the word of God, is an offensive weapon against attack.

Seek God's Wisdom

Ask God to reveal His will and guide your actions in the face of spiritual attacks.

Living in Obedience

Being obedient to God's commands involves worship, respect, rest, and reflection, which keeps you in a close relationship with God.

Morality

God requires that you do not to participate in murder, adultery, stealing, coveting, lying, and more. God requires a moral life for you. This strengthens your spiritual armor and helps you resist the enemy.

Desires

You should not be envious and desire what belongs to others or serve demons and not God.

Truth Is The Ultimate Weapon

Standing firm in the truth of The Bible, God's Word, is a powerful way to overcome the demonic lies.

Repentance and Confession

When you fall into sin or make a mistake, confess it to God, repent for the mistake or wrongdoing, and accept God's forgiveness and love.

Do Not Despair

Even in the face of spiritual attacks, remain hopeful in God's promises and trust His power.

In essence, spiritual warfare is about:

- Recognizing the reality of spiritual conflict.
- Understanding the demonic tactics and strategies.
- Reaching out to God for power and guidance.
- Living in obedience and faith.
- Relying on God's promises for victory.

Key Passages About Spiritual Warfare

Ephesians 6:10-18

This passage is a comprehensive discussion of spiritual warfare, urging believers to "put on the full armor of God" to resist the devil's schemes. It emphasizes that the battle is not against flesh and blood, but against "the rulers, the authorities, the cosmic powers over this present darkness, and the spiritual forces of evil in the heavenly places."

2 Corinthians 10:4-5

This passage highlights the weapons of spiritual warfare, which are not physical, but "mighty before God" to demolish strongholds and take captive every thought. It emphasizes the need to resist arguments and pretenses that set themselves up against the knowledge of God.

Revelation

This book contains descriptions of cosmic battles, including the war between Michael and his angels against the dragon and his angels, and the ultimate victory of Christ over evil.

James 4:7

This verse encourages submission to God and resistance to the devil, emphasizing the importance of spiritual vigilance and seeking God's grace.

Romans 8:37

This passage assures believers of victory through Christ, stating that you are "more than conquerors" in all your struggles.

1 Peter 5:8-9

This passage warns against being tempted by Satan and urges believers to remain alert and sober-minded.

Isaiah 54:17

This verse promises that no weapon formed against believers will prosper, and that they will refute every tongue that accuses them.

What Are Demonic Footholds?

Spiritual Footholds are situations, circumstances, or patterns of behavior that offer an opportunity for demonic influence to enter your life. "Satanic footholds" are a secure, strategic position from which demons can advance. These footholds can be seen as areas where Satan can enter and exert his influence. Satan and his demons gain influence over you through various actions and attitudes, and these actions and attitudes create opportunities for him to exert his power. It is like being pulled down into the unknown depths of despair and doubt. In his distress, the psalmist cried out to God for salvation. "I sink in the murky depths, where there is no foothold. I have come into the deep waters; the floods engulf me." *Psalm 69:2.*

As a Christian, Satan is looking to establish a strategic position in your life through something as simple as holding on to anger, grudges, and bitterness, etc. Once Satan establishes a foothold, He is always finding ways to make further advances into your life. He will continue to spread his lies and multiple temptations; if unchecked, his foothold can become a Stronghold. If you give Satan a foothold in your life, he will have an easier time attacking you, as he tries to separate you from God. The more footholds and the strongest foothold will eventually become a Spiritual Stronghold. Spiritual Strongholds are habitual thought patterns or mental fortresses that can prevent you from growing in your faith and living according to God's will. "And do not give the devil a foothold." *Ephesians 4:27.*

Addressing satanic footholds is seen as a part of spiritual warfare. It is a process of resisting the influence of evil forces and seeking God's protection and strength. Understanding the concept of demonic footholds and choosing to prevent and remove any footholds allows you to turn from guilt and shame. This is the end of these footholds in your life. Paul says the best way to deal with these negative emotions is to address them immediately. This stands true for all negative emotions. "Do not let the sun go down while you are still angry, for anger gives a foothold to the devil." *Ephesians 4:26b-27.*

How Do We Go About Giving Demons A Foothold?

Should you engage in certain negative behaviors, thoughts, attitudes, or sins, you can inadvertently provide demons opportunities to gain footholds in your life. Unresolved issues or persistent sins can create vulnerabilities that demons can exploit, allowing demons to influence your mind, body, and emotions.

Footholds Entry Points

Footholds entry points can include negative actions like unforgiveness, anger, resentment, bitterness, gossip, lust, pride, persistent sin, and lack of faith in God. Negative emotions and behaviors allow demons an entry point. There are situations, circumstances, or patterns of behavior that provide opportunities for demonic influence to enter into your life.

The Impact of Footholds

By allowing these things to take root, you open yourself up to further influence and spiritual harm from Satan. Once a foothold is established, demons will make the situation worse, leading to more severe spiritual problems like mental and emotional distress, addictions, or even physical ailments.

Breaking Footholds

Recognizing and addressing footholds through prayer, repentance, confession of sins, seeking God's guidance, and Deliverance can help break these demonic footholds. So, you can reclaim spiritual freedom in your life.

Generational Foothold

Negative patterns of behavior or sin can be passed down through generations, creating generational footholds that need to be addressed. "The Lord will by no means clear the guilty, but will visit the iniquity of the fathers on the children and on the grandchildren, to the third and fourth generation." *Exodus 34:7.*

At the moment of conversion, Christians are enlisted in a spiritual army and are involved in a spiritual war. They immediately become an enemy of

Satan, *Ephesians 6:10-12*. Paul warns you against giving the devil a foothold: "Do not let the sun go down while you are still angry, and do not give the devil a foothold" *Ephesians 4:26–27.*

What Are Demonic Strongholds?

The word 'strongholds' is found once in the New Testament. It is used symbolically by Paul in a description of the Christian's spiritual battle: "For though we live in the world, we do not wage war as the world does. The weapons we fight with are not the weapons of the world. On the contrary, they have divine power to demolish strongholds. We demolish arguments and every pretension that sets itself up against the knowledge of God, and we take captive every thought to make it obedient to Christ.

"Though we walk in the flesh, we do not war according to the flesh, for the weapons of our warfare are not of the flesh, but divinely powerful for the destruction of fortresses [strongholds]" *2 Corinthians 10:3-5.*

Spiritual strongholds are habitual thought patterns or mental fortresses that hinder your growth in faith and your ability to live according to God's will. These are often rooted in lies or negative beliefs that have become deeply ingrained, making it difficult to break free from them. They can manifest as limiting perceptions, negative emotions, dysfunctional behaviors, or a resistance to change. Spiritual Strongholds of Believers are like fortified areas of the emotions, the mind, and the body. Spiritual Strongholds of Non-Believers include the mind, emotions, body, and soul. Strongholds actively resist God's truth and hinder spiritual growth.

Spiritual Strongholds are often described as harmful thought patterns or beliefs that hinder your growth and relationship with God. Spiritual strongholds are persistent, often subconscious thought patterns or beliefs that hinder spiritual growth. They can lead to harmful behaviors. Strongholds are mental, spiritual barriers that hinder spiritual growth and prevent individuals from living according to God's will. Recognizing and breaking these strongholds through truth, prayer, and spiritual warfare is essential for experiencing true freedom and an abundant life.

Strongholds are not demons themselves, but demonic forces can operate within them. Strongholds developed by demonic interference influence habitual ways of thinking and behaving that create mental and emotional barriers to God's work in your life. Even though Strongholds are not demons themselves, demons can operate within them and can lead to negative behaviors and outcomes. Strongholds are places where ungodly influences can take root and thrive. Demons can keep you from thinking, accepting the truth, repeating sin, and receiving Deliverance. Strongholds can manifest as confusion, fear, anger, and unforgiveness. Strongholds manifest in many other forms.

Strongholds can develop with repeated exposure to negative thoughts, unbiblical false beliefs, harmful behavior, negative childhood experiences, societal pressure, and personal choices. Also, disobeying God's Word, disregarding His counsel, and dwelling on self-worship. Recognizing strongholds often involves identifying recurring patterns of thought or behavior that are difficult to change, even when they contradict God's truth.

How Do We Go About Breaking Spiritual Strongholds?

Overcoming Strongholds requires a committed effort to identify and dismantle all of these negative patterns of your thinking and behavior. It can be helped through Deliverance, and it can be achieved through prayer, study of God's Word, seeking guidance from trusted spiritual mentors, and practicing forgiveness and humility. Breaking off Strongholds involves replacing the lies with truth, false beliefs with God's truth, and negative habits with healthy choices.

What Are Warning Signs of Demonic Intrusion?

Attacks in your Dreams

Demons are after your peace, and one of the ways they attack you is through sleep, such as sexual dreams, evil persuasion, seeing death, or even having a dead relative or person visit. All of these are examples of demonic activity infiltrating your sleep. "But while everyone was sleeping, his enemy came and sowed weeds and went away…" *Matthew 13:25*.

The enemy is after your peace. When you cannot sleep, you are restless and tired. This negatively affects your productivity in the Kingdom of God.

Mental Oppression

Satan intrudes the mind with bad, misleading thoughts, such as worthlessness, failure, no one likes me, confusion, and many more. The mind and emotions are the battlefield, and the biggest challenge for a Believer and non-Believer is understanding that those thoughts are NOT your own. When you notice thoughts or emotions that are controlling, negative, and very persistent, you must declare war against them. Any thought of unforgiveness, loneliness, self-destruction, or a sense of "I can't control this," plus many others, are all clear indications you could be being influenced by Demons. The Bible is clear that we were given a sound mind. "If you do not choose to join with God to remove the root cause, the demon will infect your mind." *2 Timothy 1:7*.

Controlling Negative Emotions

Depression, anxiety, heaviness, rejection, resentment, unforgiveness, disappointment, loneliness, misery, self-destruction, and suicide are all potential signs of demonic activity and presence. The Bible says that these feelings are not from God. "Be anxious for nothing, but in everything by prayer and supplication, with thanksgiving, let your requests be made known to God." *Philippians 4:6*.

"For God has not given us a spirit of fear, but of power and of love and of a sound mind." *2 Timothy 1:7*.

"To console those who mourn in Zion, to give them beauty for ashes, the oil of joy for mourning, the garment of praise for the spirit of heaviness; that they may be called trees of righteousness, the planting of the Lord, that He may be glorified." *Isaiah 61:3.*

An Intense Desire for Defiled Things

It is natural for Demons to crave what is unholy and impure. If you struggle with alcohol, drugs, strong lustful thoughts, adultery, lying, stealing, gambling, etc., it is an indicator that something inside is causing you to crave something that can hurt you and others. These demons mainly manifest in addictions or sins that people cannot stop falling into. This is usually followed by shame, guilt, feelings of hate and anger, and an inability to forgive yourself.

You Cannot Contain Your Tongue

One of the signs you are filled with the Holy Spirit is that you can speak in tongues. One of the ways you can tell you are filled with demons is an impure mouth. Oftentimes, a clear indicator of demon intrusion is when someone has uncontrollable bursts of rage and is not able to stop cursing, gossiping, or blaspheming. Speaking bad or evil things against God, Christianity, and the Church is also a sign.

Sexual Perversion

Any desire for illicit sex, masturbation, a desire to commit adultery, pornography, or any form of sexual perversion can be an indicator of demonic influence.

Involvement In the Occult

Any spirituality that is not rooted in the Holy Bible is a warning sign of the demonic. Dabbling in any sort of divination, tarot cards, astrology, Eight Ball, Dungeons and Dragons, Yoga, Pokémon, and Harry Potter, Spiritual Enlightenment, etc., is an open door for demonic presence.

False Religions

In the words of Jesus, "I am the way and the truth and the life. No one comes to the Father except through me." *John 14:6*. False religions open you up to the demonic influence. False religion is anything that says there are many ways to heaven. Jesus is not the only way. Some examples are Witchcraft, Masons, Eastern Star, Satanism, Voodoo, Wicca, Hinduism, Buddhism, other gods, etc. Anything that opposes Jesus' teachings.

Chronic Sickness

The Bible shows you clear examples where sickness was the result of a demonic presence. Like Peter's mother; Jesus rebuked the fever and it left her. *Matthew 8:14-15*. The boy who had epilepsy. *Luke 9:40-44*. The boy who was mute and had seizures. After rebuking it, the spirit left him and the boy was made well. *Mark 9:17-25*.

Compulsive Behavior

When you have constant and sudden urges of rage or hostility, this can also be a sign of demons. In the Bible, Saul experienced these torments and would later be repentant of his rage. *1 Samuel 18*.

Extreme Restlessness in a Spiritual Environment

When you notice extreme tiredness when reading the Bible, praying, fasting, or during worship, this could be evidence of demons. *Thessalonians 5:6*, When a Christian gets strengthened, demons get expelled, so the demons will do anything they can to prevent that.

A Compulsive Desire to Hurt the Body

There was a man who was possessed by an evil spirit; he would cut himself with stones. Although the Bible states he had demons, it is also clear that they were unable to stop him from running to the feet of Jesus. His thoughts and actions were almost completely controlled, but He made a willful choice to run to Jesus. *Mark 5:2*. It is important to note that any thought of self-harm, harm to others, or suicide is influenced by demons.

Hearing Voices

Another clear indicator is if you are hearing voices. Especially if they refer to themselves as "us", "we", "they, "them", or if they give you a sense of evil, harm, fear, or any negative emotion, there is a demonic presence. Just remember, God does not give negative feelings; only demons do.

Paranormal Experiences

Any supernatural activity like the disappearance of objects, strange things moving in your home, feelings of fear or control without reason, strange noises, or any other strange manifestations can be clear evidence that demons are influencing your surroundings.

What To Do?

Demons are powerfully real. They wreak more havoc in your life and society. Their havoc is more than you can imagine. To counter this, you need to take God's words seriously. You need to know God. You need to believe in and follow Jesus and be Baptized in His name. The more you know God and His word and the more you trust Him and live in obedience to Him, the wiser you become and the stronger you are against demonic attack. Strive to understand, become, and do what is good, so that you can recognize what is evil. You can become a more dangerous threat to demons than they are to you. Once more, listen to God and worship Him, and become more discerning about good and evil. You can learn how to take action when faced with a demonic attack. Remember, God is light – Evil is darkness. "The God of peace will soon crush Satan under your feet. The grace of our Lord Jesus be with you." *Romans 16:20.*

"For those who are led by the Spirit of God are the children of God." *Romans 8:14.* Take time to notice the things you are constantly led to. Whatever you are filled with will lead you. If you have noticed any of these signs in your life, you need to sever any ties the demons have and pray against every demon influencing your life. The Bible instructs us how to send devils scurrying away in fear, it says,

"Submit yourselves therefore to God. Resist the devil, and he will flee from you". This is powerful spiritual warfare. *James 4:7.*

We grant authority to whomever we trust. The devil has no authority over any Christian, except the authority we grant him by believing him. The more we believe him, the more influence and control over us we give him, and the more he gets a hold on us. This is the way demons influence or control our lives, as well as any relationship we have. When it comes to demons, we do not need to claim any authority over them. Words do not act like spells with demons, *Acts 19:15.*

Demons only recognize God's authority, and they tremble before it. When we submit ourselves to God, we come under His authority by trusting, obeying, and following Him. Demons do not work well in that environment, so they tend to stay away from us. This does not mean that they may not try to influence us. We must be vigilant in our walk with God. This act of faith releases great spiritual power, and demons cannot withstand it. The more we know God and His word, the more we trust and obey Him, the more dangerous we become to Satan. *James 2:19.*

Deliverance Ministry is an effective way of casting out demons, their constant lies, and their negative influences in your life. All of this is done through the power of Jesus Christ, as negative thought patterns are broken and lies are overtaken by truth. It is time for you to turn to the Bible for God's truth. Also, turning to God allows Him to walk with you as the Strongholds that have been tormenting you are broken off.

Without Demon influences, you are more likely to make the right choice by allowing Jesus to help you. He will provide you with the strength and determination to follow Him. God is the ultimate authority over Strongholds and provides all the power to break them. Through God's Word and grace, guidance by the Holy Spirit, and salvation found through Jesus Christ, you, as a believer, are empowered to overcome these mental, emotional, and spiritual barriers. You can live the life of peace, joy, and love.

How Do You Ward Off Personal Demonic Attack?

To ward off a perceived demonic attack, focus on strengthening your spiritual defenses through faith, prayer, Bible study, worship, and seeking God's protection. Additionally, if needed, seek guidance, support, and instruction from proven and trusted Deliverance Ministers or your Pastor.

Prayer and Faith

Make prayer a daily practice of seeking God's protection and deliverance from spiritual oppression. Spend time in conversation with God to strengthen your resolve.

Spiritual Vigilance

If you feel you are being spiritually attacked, remain steadfast in your faith and heighten your spiritual awareness in your own life. God is with you. There is no reason to fear when you turn to Him. Remember, as a Christian, you have the power of Jesus Christ on your side and the Holy Spirit dwelling within you. You are wise to remain alert to potential danger and to remain strong in your faith in God. Spiritual attack is the way demons evaluate a potential victim. This is a time to review your thoughts, feelings, and actions. Also, it helps you to strengthen your discernment and resilience in the face of challenges. All of this causes you to become aware of potential spiritual attacks, and it cultivates a stronger relationship with God.

Scripture

To strengthen your faith in God, read and study the Bible regularly and rely on its teachings. Meditating on the Bible will help you understand the Word of God more clearly, and it is a powerful defense against demonic attack.

Spiritual Discipline

Maintain a life of avoiding sinful actions and things, such as drugs, out-of-wedlock sex, and profane movies, books, music, art, videos, etc. All of these ways allow demons to enter.

Repent and Forgive

When you are having negative thoughts, actions, and temptations, they can be caused by demons attacking you. Demons always lie and always present negative thoughts and behavior to you. If you believe you are experiencing demonic influence, immediately repent for any sinful thoughts and actions you have committed. Earnestly ask God for forgiveness and then accept His forgiveness. In the future, you should not listen to these thoughts, actions, or temptations. If they should come creeping back, repent, ask God to forgive you, and accept God's grace of forgiveness. We all sin. As soon as you identify the sin you have committed, repent, ask for forgiveness, and accept the Grace of God's forgiveness.

Fasting

Christian fasting is a spiritual practice that can be a powerful tool while you are seeking God through worship, the Bible, meditation, and prayer. Fasting can help focus your mind and heart on God, making it easier to hear His voice and receive His guidance.

Meditation

Meditation involves reflecting on the Bible, the Word of God. This allows God's truth and direction to saturate your heart and mind. This allows God to replace your thoughts with His thoughts, giving you the ability to receive His transformative power in your life. By being quiet, it often lets you hear Him more clearly.

Seeking Guidance

If you are struggling, consult a Godly Pastor, Spiritual Mentor, or Deliverance Minister for more personalized advice and support. Do not hesitate to ask for guidance, as everyone needs guidance. "If any of you lacks wisdom, let him ask God, who gives generously to all without reproach, and it will be given him." *James 1:5.*

Removing Negative Influences

After your Deliverance, if you believe negative influences are attracting you, such as temptation, demonic obsession, and demonic influence, remove all the items from your environment that would support these negative demonic influences. These include harmful music, books, pagan symbols, art, jewelry, movies, TV shows, games, etc. Anything that does not bring you closer to God.

Submit Yourself To Jesus

It is by the name of Jesus Christ that demons show fear and will flee. Should you need to cast out demons that are troubling you, do so through your faith in the power of Jesus' name.

Repent Of Any Sin You Have Committed

Sin is a way for demons to get or maintain control of your life. Therefore, repent of any sin and pray to God, asking for His forgiveness for your sins. Then accept the Grace that God offers you. Now is the time to forgive everyone in your life who has hurt you, lied to you, or disappointed you. This includes all organizations and institutions that have caused negative feelings, hurt, or pain in your life. Anyone or anything from your childhood to the present that has hurt you or made you feel bad—remember, forgiveness is not about condoning or forgetting the wrongs done to you. No one can earn forgiveness. It is an act of God's grace. The forgiveness you give others may not be deserved. Remember your forgiveness is choosing to extend the same forgiveness that God gave you through Jesus on the Cross. "Be kind and compassionate to one another, forgiving each other, just as in Christ God forgave you." *Ephesians 4:32,* "When you forgive others, you can find freedom."

Say out loud:

I choose to forgive _____.

Keep saying the name of another person or institution until you do not remember any more names. Do not forget yourself. If you cannot think of the name, say "that person". You know and God knows who you are talking about.

Say out loud:

I choose to forgive myself.

Accept God's grace of forgiveness, even if we think we do not deserve it or have not earned it. Thank God for His mercy to you.

Pray For Those Who Hurt You

Do not pray for what you think they should do. Pray for God to give them everything they need to live a happy, peaceful, and Godly life.

Demon Influence In Your Life

When you feel a demon presence in your life, declare: "I am a Child of God. You have no place or authority in my life. Through the name of Jesus Christ, I command you to leave and to go immediately and directly to the Abyss."

They will flee. They cannot stand firm against the power of the Lord Jesus Christ. When you feel a change from feelings of concern or fear to peace, that is a good indication they are gone.

Demons are always looking for a way in. Even though they have already lost the war, they also know they have a short time to steal souls from God and to cause havoc in the world.

Jesus told you, "Fear not for I am with you", so rely on Him. Should the demons return at any time, repeat the statement of authority, for as many times as you need. If you ever feel oppressed by any demon, get in touch with your Deliverance Minister or Pastor for guidance.

Note:

Demons cannot influence you unless you invite them back into your life through sin or lack of faith. This is why immediately repenting, asking for forgiveness, and accepting God's grace are so important. We all make mistakes. The only way to be free of these mistakes is through God. Personal prayer, reading the Bible, meditating, and playing Christian music can be helpful in this process. Just be assured, demons are already defeated and have no independent authority over you, a Christian. They can only gain authority in your life through your bad actions and thoughts, or Generational Curses.

What Makes Demons Leave?

Demons flee from God's authority, particularly when you submit to God, trust in Him, and obey His word. Demons tremble at the name of Jesus. This submission and faith release a holy power that demons cannot withstand.

God's Presence

Demons flee from God's presence due to their fear of Christ, the power of the Holy Spirit, and the authority of God's Word. They also fear judgment and wrath, and they are reminded of their ultimate destination, the Abyss.

Fear Of Christ

In the Bible, demons are depicted as recognizing and fearing Jesus' authority, often fleeing at His command or the mention of His name, as seen in passages like *Mark 1:23-26* and *Luke 4:41*.

Demons are said to know Christ's identity and are terrified by it. Demons recognize the end of their reign and the restoration of the world that Christ's presence brings. When Jesus is present and working in your life, light overcomes darkness, and demons must flee.

Prayer and Authority

Prayer, especially prayers and commands in the name of Jesus Christ, is a way to command demons to leave. In Deliverance Ministry, a very important part is to use faith, spiritual authority, and the name of Jesus Christ to command the demon to leave. The demon has no recourse but to leave.

Spiritual Warfare

In spiritual warfare, demons flee from you when you are submitting to God and actively resisting Satan's influence. This resistance is often described as standing firm in faith, relying on God's strength, and actively engaging in spiritual warfare against the demons. Engaging in spiritual warfare, which includes faith, prayer, resisting evil influences, and putting on the

Armor of God, protects Christians from demonic intrusion. It gives you power and strength to ward off evil.

Submission to God's Authority

Demons acknowledge and are subject to God's authority, recognizing His power and fearing His presence. This is evident in their trembling before God: "You believe that God is one; you do well. Even the demons believe, and shudder!" *James 2:19*. Demons are aware of God's authority and dominion over all things. Your personal submission to God's authority, through faith and obedience, is a key aspect of resisting demonic influence. "Submit yourselves, then, to God. Resist the devil, and he will flee from you." *James 4:7-8*.

When you submit to God and are Baptized, live a Christian life, worshipping and accepting Jesus Christ as your Lord and Savior, you will become closer to God. By striving to live a Christ-like life, you can depend on the Holy Spirit for guidance and for God's protection and forgiveness.

Trust and Obedience

Trusting in God and obeying His word is a core Christian belief. It is a powerful act that strengthens your spiritual life and makes you less vulnerable to demonic influence. Demons, as spiritual beings, are opposed to God and recognize His authority, but they do not obey God. Demons acknowledge God's existence and power. They fear and tremble at the name of Jesus. Your faith in God involves personal trust and obedience, which prevents Demons from leading you away from God.

The Power of Prayer

With fervent, surrendered prayer, you can align yourself with God's will and release the spiritual power given to you through the Holy Spirit. Prayer is seen as a powerful tool in spiritual warfare, including overcoming demonic influence. Through prayer, you can call upon God's power to cast out demons and break their influence. Prayer is a form of spiritual defense, seeking protection and deliverance from evil spirits.

The Name of Jesus

Demons flee at the mention of Jesus' name. The Bible does not explicitly state that demons will simply flee at the mere sound of the name Jesus. The power of the name lies in the authority and God's presence it represents, not just the words themselves. The name of Jesus has the power to command demons to flee. "And these signs will accompany those who believe: In my name they will cast out demons". *Mark 16:17*. "She kept this up for many days. Finally, Paul became so annoyed that he turned around and said to the spirit, "In the name of Jesus Christ I command you to come out of her!" At that moment the spirit left her." *Acts 16:18*.

What Is The Christian Response to The Demonic?

Demons are bent on destruction. Because the demons are fallen and evil, they are under the judgment of God. Jesus Christ will finally judge all evil, including the evil of Satan and his demons. They will be thrown into the lake of fire forever. *Revelation 20:7-10.*

How can you guard yourself against their attacks? What is your ultimate hope amid real spiritual warfare and demonic activity?

- Read and study what the Bible has to say about demons and the spiritual world.
- Acknowledge that the struggle is real and intense. You are engaged in a struggle that is bigger than flesh and blood.
- God claims every part of this world as His. Satan and his demons oppose God's work at every step.
- The work of demonic powers is constant, and it is important that you do not act as if this work does not exist. You need to be aware of the demons' deception.
- It is good for you to be on guard against the lies of Satan and his demons. John calls believers to test the spirits "Beloved, do not believe every spirit, but test the spirits to see whether they are from God, for many false prophets have gone out into the world." *1 John 4:* Deception is one of their primary functions. Demons delight in deceiving people with words and teachings that are opposed to the life-giving word of Jesus Christ.
- Jesus Christ is the Son of God sent to be the Savior of all who believe. By turning you away from Jesus, Demons are constantly pursuing the deception and destruction of all mankind. So, you need to be watchful and rely on God's love and power.

- Remember God's power. John's warning to Christians is about testing the spirits. "He who is in you is greater than He who is in the world." *1 John 4:4.*

Following Jesus Christ and the Holy Spirit dwelling in you, His power and might far outweigh that of the most powerful demon, even Satan himself. Jesus can kill the efforts of Satan and his demons with just a word. His power terrifies demons. While we need to acknowledge the power of evil in the world, we should never think it compares to the power of Jesus Christ, the risen Lord.

As you consider the demons' works, their lies, evil, and attacks in this world, you can take comfort in the fact that there will be a final Judgment. Jesus will return to this earth as the Judge and will make all things right. Satan and his demons will be thrown into the lake of fire. *Revelation 20:10.*

Death and sin will finally be defeated, and God's people will dwell with Him in a new heaven and new earth that is free from the influence of sin and evil. Today and every day, the power of God is on your side. He equips you so you can join Him in this form of spiritual warfare. He protects you from Evil, and He has allowed you the privilege of casting out demons, not only from your own life, but also from the lives of others.

Bible, Prayers, and Spiritual Warfare

What Does the Bible Say About Spiritual Warfare?

There are two primary errors when it comes to spiritual warfare: over-emphasis and under-emphasis.

Some blame every sin, every conflict, and every problem on demons that need to be cast out. Others completely ignore the spiritual realm and the fact that the Bible describes your battle as against spiritual powers. The key to successful spiritual warfare is finding a balance. Demons are not under every rock, but they are committed to their task of stealing souls from God.

The Apostle Paul Instructs Christians To Wage War Against The Sin In Themselves

Romans 6

"What shall we say, then? Shall we go on sinning so that grace may increase? By no means! We are those who have died to sin; how can we live in it any longer? Or don't you know that all of us who were baptized into Christ Jesus were baptized into His death? We were therefore buried with Him through baptism into death in order that, just as Christ was raised from the dead, through the glory of the Father, we too may live a new life. For if we have been united with Him in a death like His, we will certainly also be united with Him in a resurrection like His. For we know that our old self was crucified with Him so that the body ruled by sin might be done away with, that we should no longer be slaves to sin— because anyone who has died has been set free from sin. Now if we died with Christ, we believe that we will also live with Him. For we know that since Christ was raised from the dead, He cannot die again; death no longer has mastery over Him. The death He died, He died to sin once for all; but the life He lives, He lives to God. In the same way, count yourselves dead to sin but alive to God in Christ Jesus. Therefore, do not let sin reign in your mortal body so that you obey its evil desires. Do not offer any part of yourself to sin as an instrument of wickedness, but rather offer yourselves to God as those who have been brought from death to life; and offer every part of yourself to Him as an instrument of righteousness. For sin shall no longer be your master, because you are not under the law, but under grace. What then? Shall we sin because we are not under the law but under grace? By no means! Don't you know that when you offer yourselves to someone as obedient slaves, you are slaves of the one you obey—whether you are slaves to sin, which leads to death, or to obedience, which leads to righteousness? But thanks be to God that, though you used to be slaves to sin, you have come to obey from your heart the pattern of teaching that has now claimed your allegiance. You have been set free from sin and have become slaves to righteousness. I am using an example from everyday life because of your human limitations. Just as you used to offer yourselves as slaves to impurity and to ever-increasing wickedness, so now offer yourselves as slaves to righteousness leading to holiness. When you were slaves to sin, you were free from the control of righteousness. What benefit did you reap at that time from the things you are now ashamed of? Those things result in death! But now that you have been set free from sin and have become slaves of God, the benefit you reap leads to holiness, and the result is eternal life. For the wages of sin is death, but the gift of God is eternal life in Christ Jesus our Lord."

The Bible Also Warns You to Oppose the Schemes of Satan

Ephesians 6:10–18.

"Finally, be strong in the Lord and in His mighty power. Put on the full armor of God so that you can take your stand against the devil's schemes. For our struggle is not against flesh and blood, but against the rulers, against the authorities, against the powers of this dark world and against the spiritual forces of evil in the heavenly realms." This text teaches some crucial truths: we can only stand strong in the Lord's power, it is God's armor that protects us, and our battle is ultimately against spiritual forces of evil in the world."

This describes the spiritual armor God gives us. "Therefore put on the full armor of God, so that when the day of evil comes, you may be able to stand your ground, and after you have done everything, to stand. Stand firm then, with the belt of truth buckled around your waist, with the breastplate of righteousness in place, and with your feet fitted with the readiness that comes from the gospel of peace. In addition to all this, take up the shield of faith, with which you can extinguish all the flaming arrows of the evil one. Take the helmet of salvation and the sword of the Spirit, which is the word of God praying at all times in the Spirit, with all prayer and supplication. To that end, keep alert with all perseverance..." *Ephesians 6:13–18.*

When Entering Spiritual Warfare, Realize:

- Spiritual Armor is to be used in spiritual warfare.
- Know God's truth, believe God's truth, and speak God's truth.
- You are to declare and to live a righteous life because of Christ's sacrifice for you.
- Proclaim the Gospel and its truth.
- Do not waver in your faith; trust the promises God made to you.

As a Christian, your ultimate defense is your salvation, and no demonic power can steal that from you. In Spiritual Warfare, the offensive weapon is the Word of God, as shown in the Bible.

Jesus is our ultimate example of resisting temptation in spiritual warfare. Look at how Jesus handled direct attacks from Satan when He was tempted in the wilderness. "Then Jesus was led by the Spirit into the wilderness to be tempted by the devil. After fasting forty days and forty nights, he was hungry. Satan came to him and said, "If you are the Son of God, tell these stones to become bread." Jesus answered, 'It is written: 'Man shall not live on bread alone, but on every word that comes from the mouth of God.' Then the devil took him to the holy city and had him stand on the highest point of the temple. 'If you are the Son of God," he said, "throw yourself down. For it is written: "'He will command his angels concerning you, and they will lift you up in their hands, so that you will not strike your foot against a stone.' Jesus answered him, "It is also written: 'Do not put the Lord your God to the test.' Again, the devil took him to a very high mountain and showed him all the kingdoms of the world and their splendor. 'All this I will give you," he said, 'if you will bow down and worship me." Jesus said to him, 'Away from me, Satan! For it is written: 'Worship the Lord your God, and serve Him only.' Then the devil left Him, and angels came and attended Him." *Matthew 4:1–11*. The Bible is the most powerful weapon against the temptations of the devil. "I have hidden your word in my heart that I might not sin against you." *Psalm 119:11*.

A word of caution concerning spiritual warfare. You are only human, and all authority comes from God. An example of what can happen when people presume an authority they have not been given. "Some Jews who went around driving out evil spirits tried to invoke the name of the Lord Jesus over those who were demon-possessed. They would say, "In the name of the Jesus whom Paul preaches, I command you to come out." Seven sons of Sceva, a Jewish chief priest, were doing this. One day, the evil spirit answered them, "Jesus I know, and Paul I know about, but who are you?" Then the man who had the evil spirit jumped on them and overpowered them all. He gave them such a beating that they ran out of the house naked and bleeding. *Acts 19:13-16*.

It is important to note that the seven sons of a Jewish High Priest were not Christians, who called on the name of Jesus. Without belief and faith in the Lord Jesus Christ, believing He is the Son of God, and through Jesus, the authority to cast out demons is given, they had no power against the demons they were trying to cast out. All power and authority to cast out demons comes from God.

Pray directly to God the Father, God the Son, and God the Holy Spirit each day. It is through God that all your protection comes. Do not have a conversation directly with the demon; you run the risk of being led astray, as Eve was. You are mortal and need the power of our Lord Jesus Christ to deal directly with all demons.

"Now the serpent was craftier than any of the wild animals the Lord God had made. He said to the woman, "Did God really say, 'You must not eat from any tree in the garden'? The woman said to the serpent, 'We may eat fruit from the trees in the garden, but God did say, 'You must not eat fruit from the tree that is in the middle of the garden, and you must not touch it, or you will die. You will not certainly die," the serpent said to the woman. 'For God knows that when you eat from it your eyes will be opened, and you will be like God, knowing good and evil.' When the woman saw that the fruit of the tree was good for food and pleasing to the eye, and also desirable for gaining wisdom, she took some and ate it. She also gave some to her husband, who was with her, and he ate it. Then the eyes of both of them were opened, and they realized they were naked; so they sewed fig leaves together and made coverings for themselves." *Genesis 3:1–7.*

You submit to God's will. Keep your focus on God, not demons. You are loved by God, protected by the Holy Spirit, and through the power of the Lord Jesus Christ, you are given the ability to perform His will in the world.

The Keys To Success In Spiritual Warfare

- Rely on God's power, not our own.
- Put on the whole Armor of God. The Armor of God protects you from harm that could be caused by Demons. The power of The Sword of the Spirit, the word of God, is used for defending against and attacking demons. Never take off your armor. You can check your spiritual well-being each day to make sure your armor is strapped on tightly.
- Stand firm with others. "Therefore put on the full armor of God, so that when the day of evil comes, you may be able to stand your ground, and after you have done everything, to stand. Stand firm then, with the belt of truth buckled around your waist, with the breastplate of righteousness in place." *Ephesians 6:13–14.*
- Submit your prayers to Jesus. Never appeal directly to demons or Satan, only through Jesus – in the name of Jesus Christ. He is the one with power and authority.
- Submit to God and resist Satan's schemes. "Submit yourself, then, to God. Resist the devil, and he will flee

from you, knowing that the Lord of hosts is our protector." *James 4:7.* "Truly he is my rock and my salvation; he is my fortress, I will never be shaken". *Psalm 62:2.*

What Does Jesus Says About Dealing with Evil?

"Jesus said to him, "Again it is written, 'You shall not put the Lord your God to the test." *Matthew 4:7.*

"But I say to you that everyone who is angry with his brother will be liable to judgment; whoever insults his brother will be liable to the council; and whoever says, 'You fool!' will be liable to the hell of fire." *Matthew 5:22.*

"You have heard that it was said, 'An eye for an eye and a tooth for a tooth.' But I say to you, Do not resist the one who is evil. But if anyone slaps you on the right cheek, turn to him the other also." *Matthew 5:38-39.*

"You have heard that it was said, 'You shall love your neighbor and hate your enemy.' But I say to you, Love your enemies and pray for those who persecute you, so that you may be sons of your Father who is in heaven. For he makes his sun rise on the evil and on the good, and sends rain on the just and on the unjust. For if you love those who love you, what reward do you have? Do not even the tax collectors do the same? And if you greet only your brothers, what more are you doing than others? Do not even the Gentiles do the same? ..." *Matthew 5:43-39.*

"So whatever you wish that others would do to you, do also to them, for this is the Law and the Prophets." *Matthew 7:12.*

"And do not fear those who kill the body but cannot kill the soul. Rather fear him who can destroy both soul and body in hell." *Matthew 10:28.*

"I tell you, on the day of judgment people will give account for every careless word they speak, for by your words you will be justified, and by your words you will be condemned." *Matthew 12:36-37.*

"At that time the disciples came to Jesus, saying, 'Who is the greatest in the kingdom of heaven?" And calling to him a child, he put him in the midst of them and said, "Truly, I say to you, unless you turn and become like children, you will never enter the kingdom of heaven. Whoever humbles himself like this child is the greatest in the kingdom of heaven. "Whoever receives one such child in my name receives me," *Matthew 18:1-5.*

"If your brother sins against you, go and tell him his fault, between you and him alone. If he listens to you, you have gained your brother. But if he does not listen, take one or two others along with you, that every charge may be established by the evidence of two or three witnesses. If he refuses to listen to them, tell it to the church. And if he refuses to listen even to the church, let him be to you as a Gentile and a tax collector." *Matthew 18:15-17.*

"Just so, I tell you, there will be more joy in heaven over one sinner who repents than over ninety-nine righteous persons who need no repentance." *Luke 15:7.*

"Behold, I have given you authority to tread on serpents and scorpions, and over all the power of the enemy, and nothing shall hurt you." *Luke 10:19.*

"If you love me, you will keep my commandments." *John 14:15.*

"But the Helper, the Holy Spirit, whom the Father will send in my name, he will teach you all things and bring to your remembrance all that I have said to you." *John 14:26.*

What Does the Bible Say About the Disciples Casting Out Demons?

Casting out demons is a practice mentioned in the early days of the Bible. In the Old Testament, demons were cast out. The New Testament Gospels and the Book of Acts speak about Jesus' Birth, Ministry, Death, Resurrection, and Ascension; as well as when Jesus and His disciples are shown casting out demons. The Gospels record that Jesus "called to them his twelve disciples and gave them authority over unclean spirits, to cast them out, and to heal every disease and every infirmity" *Matthew 10:1*.

Jesus also cited demons being cast out in His name as one of the signs that would follow His disciples *Mark 16:17*. This begins to happen in Acts. Apart from some brief mentions of casting out demons, the Bible records only two detailed accounts. One is when Paul helps a slave girl who has "a spirit of Python, a spirit for foretelling the future. When Paul did this, it is reported to have used only a short command, but one augmented with the name of Jesus: "I charge you in the name of Jesus Christ to come out of her" *Acts 16:18*.

- "Then he called his twelve disciples to him and gave them authority over unclean spirits, to cast them out, and to heal every disease and every affliction." *Matthew 10:1*.
- "Then he called his twelve disciples together and gave them power and authority over all demons, and to cure diseases." *Luke 9:1*.
- "He sent them to preach the kingdom of God and to heal the sick." *Luke 9:2*.
- "And that they should have power to heal, and to cast out devils" *Mark 3:15*.
- "Master," said John, "we saw someone driving out demons in your name and we tried to stop him, because he is not one of us." "Do not stop him," Jesus said, "for whoever is not against you is for you." As the time approached for Him to be taken up to heaven, Jesus resolutely set out for

Jerusalem. And He sent messengers on ahead, who went into a Samaritan village to get things ready for Him; but the people there did not welcome Him, because He was heading for Jerusalem. When the disciples James and John saw this, they asked, "Lord, do you want us to call fire down from heaven to destroy them[a]?" But Jesus turned and rebuked them." *Luke 9:49-55.*

- "He called his twelve disciples together and gave them power and authority over all demons, and to cure diseases. He sent them to preach the kingdom of God and to heal the sick." *Luke 9:1-2.*
- "Heal the sick, raise the dead, cleanse the lepers, and cast out demons. Freely you have received, freely give." Matthew 10:8. "so that even handkerchiefs and aprons that had touched him were taken to the sick, and their illnesses were cured and the evil spirits left them." *Acts 19:12.*
- "These signs will accompany those who believe in my name they drive out demons." *Mark 16:17.*

It appears the purpose of Jesus' disciples performing Deliverance/Exorcism was to show Christ's dominion over the demons *Luke 10:17*, and to verify the disciples were acting in His name and by His authority. It also revealed their faith or lack of faith. *Matthew 17:14-21*. It was obvious that this act of casting out demons was important to the ministry of the disciples.

There seems to be a shift later in the New Testament regarding demonic warfare. The teaching portions of the New Testament, Romans through Jude, refer to demonic activity, yet do not discuss the actions of casting them out, nor are believers told to do so. They are told to put on the Armor of God to stand against them, *Ephesians 6:10-18.* They are told to resist Satan, *James 4:7*, be careful of him, *Peter 5:8*, and not give him room in our lives, *Ephesians 4:27*. However, it was not told how to cast Satan or his demons out of others, or that you should even consider doing this. The reason could be due to the information provided to the disciples earlier.

The book of Ephesians gives clear instructions on how you are to have victory in your life in the battle against Satan. The first step is placing our faith in Christ, Ephesians 2:8-9, which breaks the rule of "the prince of the power of the air" *Ephesians 2:2*. We are then to choose, again by God's grace, to put off ungodly habits and to put on godly habits, *Ephesians 4:17-24*. This does not involve casting out demons, but rather renewing your mind, *Ephesians. 4:23*.

After several practical instructions on how to obey God as His children, you are reminded that there is a spiritual battle. It is fought with The Armor of God that allows us to stand against—not cast out—the trickery of the demonic world *Ephesians 6:10*. We stand with truth, righteousness, faith, salvation, the Bible, and prayer *Ephesians 6:10-18*.

It could be speculated that the shift in deliverance in the latter books of the New Testament was because they did not put an emphasis on the fact that Jesus had already told His disciples to cast out demons when he sent them out in pairs for the first time. Also, they did not emphasize that Jesus delivered people from demons.

After Jesus's Crucifixion, the stories about His life were told by word of mouth. The earliest books were written within 20 years after Jesus' crucifixion. The other books of the New Testament began to be written about 45 years after His crucifixion. They concluded around 95 AD. While written by various authors during this period, the New Testament was not compiled into a single collection until the 3rd or 4th centuries.

Early Christians, inspired by Jesus's actions and teachings, have practiced Deliverance since the early days of the faith. This practice was rooted in the Bible and the teachings of Jesus. It gained importance in the second century. Origen, an early Christian theologian, wrote about how Christians used the name of Jesus to expel "evil spirits from souls and bodies", consolidating the practice within the Christian faith. Early Christians copied the casting out of demons done by Jesus and His disciples. These practices progressed through the third and fourth centuries, ultimately leading to how casting out demons was done, as found in the "Great Book of Need".

The Greek Orthodox Church has been using exorcism (deliverance) since the third century. The Catholic Church practiced exorcism long before formal guidelines were established, with evidence of exorcism rituals and beliefs dating back to the early Church. The Catholic Church sanctioned the rite of exorcism to be official, "Ritual Romanum", in 1614. The practice of exorcism and the belief that demonic possession have roots in the early church, or even before the church was formed. The first official guidelines were established in 1614. Martin Luther practiced exorcism during the 1500s, viewing it as part of the "war with the devil," and this tradition was continued by Lutherans throughout the Reformation.

The Denomination of Churches that sanction Exorcism/ Deliverance today

Church of England	Lutheran
Episcopal	Mennonites
Baptist	Methodist
Catholic	Oriental Orthodox Church
Eastern Orthodox Church	Charismatic

What Is the Role of the Holy Spirit in Spiritual Warfare?

Since his fall, Satan is working to destroy humanity through deception *John 8:44, Genesis 2:1, Genesis 2:17, Genesis 3:1-24* and *Revelation 12:12, Revelation 12:17.* Consequently, when you witness to people, you are engaging in spiritual warfare to set the captives free from spiritual bondage.

Satan's demons use different strategies to wage war against you. They use deception, temptation, accusation, negligence, rebelliousness, fear, ungodliness, etc. In fact, On your behalf, the Lord has already won the victory over sin, Satan, death, and darkness. Jesus' power enables you to live out and claim your victory over the power of the darkness.

The Battle Is Already Won

Winning the spiritual battle is accomplished "not by might, nor by power; but by God's Spirit", *Zechariah 4:6.* The Lord has already won the victory over sin, Satan, death, and darkness on behalf of us. His power is first and foremost in securing spiritual victory for you as a Christian. If you pay attention to the Holy Spirit, you will grow into spiritual maturity and secure the victory that Jesus has already won for you and the glory of your God.

In spiritual warfare, you, as a believer, play roles that involve trusting in God's power, relying on the Bible, praying, resisting temptation, actively seeking to live a life pleasing to God, engaging with spiritual disciplines, and seeking the guidance of the Holy Spirit.

The gifts of the Holy Spirit will bring forth the fullness of Jesus' ministry in your life. It is through the gifts of the Spirit that you can minister effectively to one another and receive the help of the Holy Spirit in your life. All of your spiritual gifts are used to glorify Christ and to benefit others. Not every Christian has the same gift, just as not every part of the human body performs the same function. *1 Corinthians 12:14-26.*

God desires your life to display the fruit of the Spirit. Your Christ-like character Is known by our fruit. *Matthew 7:20.* As you allow the Holy Spirit to work in your life, He will produce more and more of His fruit in you and conquer your sinful natures to transform you into God's image. The gifts of the Spirit and the fruit of the Spirit enable you to become victorious in your spiritual warfare.

Trust in God's Power

The foundation of spiritual warfare is trusting in God's power, not your own.

Embrace the Gospel

Trust in the Gospel of Jesus Christ and His victory over sin and death.

Repentance and Resistance of Temptation

Repent from sin and resist temptation, as these can provide a foothold for the enemy.

Spiritual Disciplines

Practice spiritual disciplines such as prayer, Bible study, worship, and fellowship with other believers.

Prayer

Engage in consistent prayer, both personal and with the Church, as you seek God's guidance and intervention.

Practical Actions

Examine Yourself

Regularly examine your heart and life, ensuring you are not harboring unforgiveness, unrepentant sin, or allowing a demonic foothold.

Put on the Armor of God

Embrace the spiritual armor described in *Ephesians 6*, which includes truth, righteousness, peace, faith, salvation, and prayer.

Claim God's Promises

Embrace the promises of God found in Scripture and claim them in faith.

Waging Warfare with the Sword of the Spirit

Use the Word of God (the Sword of the Spirit) as your weapon, relying on its power to destroy strongholds and reveal truth.

Cultivate Spiritual Viewpoint

Set your eyes upon Christ and cultivate spiritual viewpoints, allowing the Spirit to lead and guide your life.

Seek Wisdom and Discernment

Pray for wisdom and discernment to recognize the enemy's tactics and to respond effectively.

Partner with Other Believers

Team up with other disciples for mutual encouragement and support in spiritual warfare.

Exercise Spiritual Gifts

Use the spiritual gifts God has given you to serve others and build up the Church.

Rely on God's Power

Recognize that victory in spiritual warfare is not achieved through your strength, but through God's power.

Recognize Satan's Deception

Be aware of the enemy's tactics and seek to expose his lies and deceptions.

Be Aware of the Reality of Spiritual Warfare

Recognize that spiritual warfare is a reality and that you are not alone in this battle. Join together as one with others. *Mathew 20*, "For where two or three are gathered together in my name I am with them."

Stand Firm in Faith

Stand firm in your faith, knowing that God is with you and that He will protect you.

Remember the Victory of Christ

Remember that Jesus has already won the victory over sin and death, and that you are seated with Him in heavenly places.

Walk In the Spirit

The believer engages in spiritual warfare against the flesh by choosing to allow the Spirit to lead, guide, and direct you in all of your life. The Spirit empowers a new, transformed life for you, so that victory in spiritual battle can be realized. *Romans 8:9–13,* "So I say, walk by the Spirit, and you will not gratify the desires of the flesh." *Galatians 5:16.*

- Renewing your Mind and walking with the Spirit, so that God's beauty and love can be made real.
- You will know by how you are acting and by how others respond.
- Looking for what God has for you personally and for your missions. Not what you think He has for you, but following where He leads you.

What Is Spiritual Warfare Through Prayer and the Bible?

According to Paul, all of life is spiritual warfare. He tells us in Ephesians how important it is, and that the Armor of God is not enough. You need to be in constant contact with God. This means you stay in contact with God through prayer. *Ephesians. 6:18–20.* The Bible encourages prayer as a means to engage in spiritual warfare and access the resources God provides.

Bible Verses for Spiritual Warfare Prayer

- "No weapon forged against you will prevail." *Isaiah 54:17.*
- "For though we live in the world, we do not wage war as the world does. The weapons we fight with are not the weapons of the world." *2 Corinthians 10:35.*
- "He who dwells in the shelter of the Most High will abide in the shadow of the Almighty." *Psalm 91.*
- "Submit yourselves therefore to God. Resist the devil, and he will flee from you." *James 4:7.*
- "No weapon forged against you will prevail, and you will refute every tongue that accuses you." *Isaiah 54:17.*
- "Do not be anxious about anything, but in every situation, by prayer and petition, with thanksgiving, present your requests to God." *Philippians 4:6-7.*

Prayer Statements for Spiritual Warfare

"Strengthen my faith, Lord. Forgive my sins, so that I may be clean in your righteousness."

"Give me your wisdom and discernment so I will not be caught off guard."

"Help me to avoid temptation and deliver me from evil, Lord."

"I declare and decree that I am more than a conqueror through Jesus Christ."

"I come to Your refuge with joy for You shelter me against the attack of the devil."

"I invite you to fill me afresh today, and have complete control over my life."

"I claim in every way Your victory over all satanic forces active in my life."

"I am thankful, Heavenly Father, that the weapons of our warfare are not carnal but mighty through God to the pulling down of strongholds, to the casting down of imaginations and every high thing that exalts itself against the knowledge of God, and to bring every thought into obedience to the Lord Jesus Christ."

Prayer for Intercession in Spiritual Warfare

"Heavenly Father, I come before you today, acknowledging the spiritual battles I face. I stand firm in Your power and authority, clothed in the full Armor of God: the belt of truth, the breastplate of righteousness, the shield of faith, the helmet of salvation, and the sword of the Spirit, which is Your Word. I declare that no weapon formed against me shall prosper, and I resist every attack of the enemy in Jesus' name. I strengthen my faith. Give me discernment to recognize the schemes of Satan. Empower me to stand against every stronghold of darkness. Lord, I ask for your protection over me and my loved ones. I submit my will to yours. Thank you for providing Your victory over evil and for the assurance that I am more than a conqueror through Christ Jesus. Amen."

Prayer for Victory in Spiritual Warfare

"Heavenly Father, I come before You today with a heart overflowing with gratitude and praise. You are the Almighty God, the Lord of Hosts, my Defender, and my Deliverer. Thank You for the victory You have secured for me through Jesus Christ, my Savior and King. Lord, I praise You because in every battle, You have been my strength. When Satan came in like a flood, You lifted up a standard against him. When I felt weak and weary, Your Spirit empowered me to stand firm in faith. Thank You for breaking every chain that once held me captive and for tearing down strongholds that sought to keep me bound. Amen."

Prayer Of Thanksgiving in Spiritual Warfare

"I declare, Lord, that the weapons of my warfare are not carnal, but mighty through You. You pull down every stronghold of fear, doubt, and sin. Thank You for arming me with the belt of truth, the shield of faith, and the sword of the Spirit. Through Your Word, I have overcome the schemes of Satan and have walked in the freedom Christ purchased for me at the cross. Father, I thank You that no weapon formed against me shall prosper. Thank You for teaching my hands to war and my fingers to fight, for guiding me with wisdom, and for surrounding me with Your angels of protection.

Lord, today I stand victorious, not by my own might or power, but by Your Spirit. Thank You for the breakthroughs, the deliverance, and the restoration You have brought into my life. I want to be more than a conqueror through Christ, who loves me. May my life always reflect Your glory, and may I walk boldly in the authority You have given me. Help me to remain steadfast, watchful, and clothed in Your righteousness, knowing that You have provided me with all I need. Help me to remain steadfast, watchful, and clothed in Your righteousness, knowing that You who have begun a good work in me and help me carry it to completion. All honor, glory, and praise belong to You, Lord. In Jesus' mighty name, I give thanks and declare victory over evil. Amen."

Other Tips For Spiritual Warfare

- Put God first
- Stay close to Jesus
- Look to the Holy Spirit to unite you with Christ
- Empower Christian living
- Guide you in truth and comfort
- Pray and listen for God's direction in your life
- Read the Bible daily
- Know the real enemy
- Put on the full Armor of God
- Submit to God and resist the Devil
- Invoke the authority of Jesus
- Live out your true identity

What Is the Armor of God?

The Armor of God is given to you so that you can resist the Evil One.

"Therefore, put away all filthiness and rampant wickedness and receive with meekness the implanted word, which is able to save your souls." *James 1:21.*

"Submit yourselves therefore to God. Resist the devil, and he will flee from you." *James 4:7.*

How To Put on the Armor of God

You "put on" the Armor of God through prayer and intentional focus on the attributes and principles listed below. This involves consciously aligning your thoughts, attitudes, and actions in your daily life with these spiritual principles and relying on God's strength to help you live according to them. Regular prayer, study of the Bible, and fellowship with other believers are vital to this process. Never take your Armor off.

- Finding God by reading scripture and through prayer keeps your mind on God and not on worldly things.
- Trust God knows what is best for me.
- Be thankful for what I have been through because they changed me for the better.

The Armor of God

"Finally, be strong in the Lord and in his mighty power. Put on the full armor of God, so that you can take your stand against the devil's schemes. For our struggle is not against flesh and blood, but against the rulers, against the authorities, against the powers of this dark world and against the spiritual forces of evil in the heavenly realms. Therefore, put on the full armor of God, so that when the day of evil comes, you may be able to stand your ground, and after you have done everything, to stand. Stand firm then," *Ephesians 6:10-17.*

The Belt of Truth

Fasten the belt standing in God's truth. Identify the lies you are believing.

"Therefore, my beloved brethren whom I long to see, my joy and crown, in this way stand firm in the Lord, my beloved." *Philippians 4:1.*

"See to it that no one takes you captive by philosophy and empty deceit, according to human tradition, according to the elemental spirits of the world, and not according to Christ." *Colossians 2:8.*

"For the weapons of our warfare are not of the flesh but have divine power to destroy strongholds. We destroy arguments and every lofty opinion raised against the knowledge of God, and take every thought captive to obey Christ." *2 Corinthians 10:4-5.*

"I have been crucified with Christ. It is no longer I who live, but Christ who lives in me. And the life I now live in the flesh I live by faith in the Son of God, who loved me and gave himself for me." *Galatians 2:20.*

The Sword of the Spirit

As an offensive and defensive weapon belonging to the Holy Spirit, all Christian soldiers need the same rigid training to properly handle the Sword of the Spirit, "which is the word of God." *2 Timothy 3:16-17.*

"All Scripture is God-breathed and is useful for teaching, rebuking, correcting and training in righteousness, so that the servant of God may be thoroughly equipped for every good work." *2 Corinthians 10:4-5.*

"For the weapons of our warfare are not of the flesh but have divine power to destroy strongholds. We destroy arguments and every lofty opinion raised against the knowledge of God, and take every thought captive to obey Christ." *Hebrews 4:12.*

"For the word of God is living and active, sharper than any two-edged sword, piercing to the division of soul and of spirit, of joints and of marrow, and discerning the thoughts and Intentions of the heart." *Psalms 11:11.*

"Teach me, Lord, the way of your decrees, that I may follow it to the end. Give me understanding, so that I may keep your law and obey it with all my heart. Direct me in the path of your commands, for there I find delight. Turn my heart toward your statutes and not toward selfish gain. Turn my eyes away from worthless things; preserve my life according to your word. Fulfill your promise to our servant, so that you may be feared. Take away the disgrace I dread, for your laws are good. How I long for your precepts! In your righteousness preserve my life." *Psalms 119:33-40.*

Breastplate Of Righteousness

The Breastplate of Righteousness, in the context of biblical armor, signifies the protection afforded by righteousness. It shields our hearts and minds from the "fiery darts of the evil one" *Ephesians 6:16,* and the temptations of the world, "and be found in him, not having a righteousness of my own that comes from the law, but that which is through faith in Christ—the righteousness that comes from God on the basis of faith." *Philippians 3:9.*

"But if we walk in the light, as he is in the light, we have fellowship with one another, and the blood of Jesus his Son cleanses us from all sin." *1 John 1:17.*

"If we confess our sins, he is faithful and just and will forgive us our sins and purify us from all unrighteousness." *1 John 1:9.*

Shoes Of Peace

"The Shoes Of Peace provides you with readiness and preparation that Christians have for sharing the good news of Jesus. We standing firm in faith," as described in *Ephesians 6:15.*

This "readiness" is also about being ready to act on it in all areas of your life, including spiritual battles and everyday challenges.

"And let the peace of God rule in your hearts, to which also you were called in one body; and be thankful." *Colossians 3:15.*

"what you have learned and received and heard and seen in me – practice these things, and the God of Peace will be with you" *Philippians 4:9.*

Shield Of Faith

The Shield of Faith defends you from spiritual attack, can extinguish all the flaming arrows of the evil, and throw the enemy off guard.

"Be sober-minded; be watchful. Your adversary the devil, prowls around like a roaring lion, seeking someone to devour. Resist him, firm in your faith, knowing that the same kinds of suffering are being experienced by your brotherhood throughout the world."*1 Peter 5:8-9.*

"For by grace you have been saved through faith. And this is not your own doing; it is the gift of God." *Ephesians 2:8.*

"And whatever you ask in prayer, you will receive, if you have faith." *Matthew 21:22.*

"Is anyone among you sick? Let him call for the elders of the church, and let them pray over him, anointing him with oil in the name of the Lord. And the prayer of faith will save the one who is sick, and the Lord will raise him up. And if he has committed sins, he will be forgiven." *James:5-14-15.*

Helmet Of Salvation

Represents the hope and assurance of salvation provided by God, acting as a shield for the mind against the darkness of this world. It signifies your secure identity and protection in Christ, ensuring that you are on God's side in the spiritual battle.

"The Lord looked and was displeased that there was no justice. He saw that there was no one, he was appalled that there was no one to intervene, so his own arm achieved salvation for him, and his own righteousness sustained him. He put on righteousness as his breastplate, and the helmet of salvation on his head; he put on the garments of vengeance and wrapped himself in zeal as in a cloak." *Isaiah 59:10-17.*

But let us who are of the day be sober, and put on the armor of faith and love, and for helmet the hope of salvation." *1 Thessalonians 5:8.*

Be prepared at all times. Read, Pray, and Memorize Scripture

What Is the Prayer to Use When Putting on the Armor of God?

Dear God,

Today, I put on the full Armor of God to guard my life against attack.

I put on the Belt of Truth to protect against lies and deception.

I put on the Breastplate of Righteousness to protect our hearts from the temptations I battle.

I put on the Gospel of Peace on our feet, so we are ready to take Your light, wherever You find me this day.

I choose to walk in the peace and freedom of Your Spirit and not be overcome with fear and anxious thoughts.

I take up Your Shield of Faith that will extinguish all the darts and threats hurled our way by the enemy.

I believe in Your power to protect us and choose to trust in You.

I put on the Helmet of Salvation, which covers our minds and thoughts, reminding me I am a child of God, forgiven, set free, and saved by the grace of Christ Jesus.

I take up the Sword of the Spirit, Your very Word, and the one offensive weapon given to me for battle, which has the power to demolish strongholds, alive, active, and is sharper than any two-edged sword.

I ask for your help in remembering always to keep Your full Armor on every day, for you give me all that I need to stand firm in this world.

Forgive us God, for the time I have been unprepared, too busy to care, or trying to fight and wrestle in my own strength.

Thank you that I never fight alone, for you are constantly at work on my behalf - shielding, protecting, strengthening, exposing deeds of darkness, bringing to light what needs to be known, and covering me from the cruel attacks I face even when I am unaware. In the Power of Jesus Christ, Amen

Check Your Armor of God daily to make sure the Armor is securely on and ready for battle. Remember, this is a gift from God to protect and defend you from any harm.

Never Take Your Armor Off!

God and Spiritual Warfare

What Are Some Ways for You to Stay Close to God?

Is It from the God or the Devil?

Remember, God shows you the right path to take. He does not hide His will from those who seek Him. Ask yourself these questions as you examine whether or not the promptings you receive are from the Lord.

Is It Confusing or Vague?

God is not the author of confusion; He is the bringer of peace. "For God is not a God of confusion but of peace." *1 Corinthians 14:*

Does It Go Against God's Word?

God will not contradict Himself. Will following these promptings lead to sin? Those who live by the Spirit will not gratify the desires of the sinful nature." But I say, walk by the Spirit, and you will not gratify the desires of the flesh." *Galatians 5:16.*

Seek Counsel from A Christian Friend, Family Member, Or Pastor.

Confirm your commitment to Christ, then submit every decision you face to Him. When we sincerely seek God's will above all else, He will guide us to know what is right.

"Without counsel plans fail, but with many advisers they succeed." *Proverbs 15:22.*

"Trust in the Lord with all your heart and lean not on your own understanding; in all your ways acknowledge him, and he will make your paths straight." *Proverbs 3:5-6.*

Having Faith and Living Like Christ

"So, faith comes from hearing, and hearing through the word of Christ."

Romans 10:17.

"Love is patient and kind; love does not envy or boast; it is not arrogant or rude. It does not insist on its own way; it is not irritable or resentful; it does not rejoice at wrongdoing, but rejoices with the truth. Love bears all things, believes all things, hopes all things, endures all things. Love never ends. As for prophecies, they will pass away; as for tongues, they will cease; as for knowledge, it will pass away." *1 Corinthians 13:4-8.*

Reading and Learning from the Bible

"For the word of God is living and active, sharper than any two-edged sword, piercing to the division of soul and of spirit, of joints and of marrow, and discerning the thoughts and intentions of the heart." *Hebrews 4:12.*

"My tongue will sing of your word, for all your commandments are right." *Psalm 119:172.*

"But as for you, continue in what you have learned and have become convinced of, because you know those from whom you learned it, and how from infancy you have known the Holy Scripture, which are able to make you wise for salvation through faith in Christ Jesus. All Scripture is God-breathed and is useful for teaching, rebuking, correcting and training in righteousness, so that the servant of God may be thoroughly equipped for every good work." *2 Timothy 3:14-17.*

Seeking Advice from A Godly Mentor

"The way of a fool is right in his own eyes, but a wise man listens to advice." *Proverbs 12:15.*

Keeping A Pure Life and Living the Commandments – Old and New

"For the mind that is set on the flesh is hostile to God, for it does not submit to God's law; indeed, it cannot." *Romans 8:7.*

"In their case the god of this world has blinded the minds of the unbelievers, to keep them from seeing the light of the gospel of the glory of Christ, who is the image of God." *2 Corinthians 4:4.*

By Your Fruit It Is Known

"I am the true vine, and my Father is the vinedresser. Every branch in me that does not bear fruit he takes away, and every branch that does bear fruit he prunes, that it may bear more fruit. Already you are clean because of the word that I have spoken to you. Abide in me, and I in you. As the branch cannot bear fruit by itself, unless it abides in the vine, neither can you, unless you abide in me. I am the vine; you are the branches. Whoever abides in me and I in him, he it is that bears much fruit, for apart from me you can do nothing." *John 15:1-27.*

"For I know the plans I have for you, declares the Lord, plans for welfare and not for evil, to give you a future and a hope." *Jeremiah 29:11.*

"So, shall my word be that goes out from my mouth; it shall not return to me empty, but it shall accomplish that which I purpose, and shall succeed in the thing for which I sent it." *Isaiah 55:11.*

Bringing Salvation to Others

"Thus, says the Lord: "Keep justice, and do righteousness, for soon my salvation will come, and my deliverance be revealed. Blessed is the man who does this, and the son of man who holds it fast, who keeps the Sabbath, not profaning it, and keeps his hand from doing any evil." Let not the foreigner who has joined himself to the Lord say, "The Lord will surely separate me from his people"; and let not the eunuch say, "Behold, I am a dry tree." For thus says the Lord: "To the eunuchs who keep my Sabbaths, who choose the things that please me and hold fast my covenant, I will give in my house and within my walls a monument and a name better than sons and daughters; I will give them an everlasting name that shall not be cut off." *Isaiah 56:1-12.*

"And to bring to light for everyone what is the plan of the mystery hidden for ages in God who created all things," *Ephesians 3:9.*

How Do You Rely on God and Not Yourself?

Meet Daily with God in Humility

"For our struggle is not against flesh and blood, but against the rulers, against the authorities, against the powers of this dark world, and against the spiritual forces of evil in the heavenly realms. Therefore put on the full armor of God, so that when the day of evil comes, you may be able to stand your ground, and after you have done everything, to stand. Stand firm then, with the belt of truth buckled around your waist, with the breastplate of righteousness in place, and with your feet fitted with the readiness that comes from the gospel of peace. In addition to all this, take up the shield of faith, with which you can extinguish all the flaming arrows of the evil one. Take the helmet of salvation and the sword of the Spirit, which is the word of God." *Ephesians 6:12.*

Renounce Any Lies

Write down any lies that you are believing.

Father, are there any lies I believe about You or myself?

Father I renounce the Lie that You are_____ or I am_____

Repent And Commit

"If my people, who are called by my name, will humble themselves and pray and seek my face and turn from their wicked ways, then I will hear from heaven, and I will forgive their sin and will heal their land." *2 Chronicles 7:14.*

Father, forgive me for partnering with the Enemy and believing his lies.

Father, I commit to You, listen to You, and not walk in the steps of Satan.

Be Forgiven - Rely On God's Mercy And Grace

"All the prophets testify about Him that everyone who believes in Him receives forgiveness of sins through His name." *Acts 10:41.*

Father, I receive your great forgiveness for my life and I accept your mercy today. I forgive myself for falling short of Your plans for me, as I continue to follow You daily.

Be Grateful

"Do not be anxious about anything, but in every situation, by prayer and petition, with thanksgiving, present your requests to God." *Philippians 4:6.*

Father, what truth do you have for my heart, as I exchange any lies for the mercy and love you have shown to me?

Be Transformed

"Do not conform to the pattern of this world, but be transformed by the renewing of your mind. Then you will be able to test and approve what God's will is—his good, pleasing and perfect will." *Romans 12:2.*

"Whoever belongs to God hears what God says. The reason you do not hear is that you do not belong to God." *John 8:47.*

Father. I ask you for the power and strength to follow your will in my life.

Walk In the Spirit

"So I say, walk by the Spirit, and you will not gratify the desires of the flesh." *Galatians 5:16.*

Renewing your mind and walking in the Spirit, so that beauty can be manifest.
Father, I ask You to help me know Your purpose for my life. Not just what I think You want me to do, but how I can serve You better.

Meet Daily with God in Humility

Write down any lies that you are believing that separate you from God.

Renounce

Father, are there any lies I believe about You, others and myself?

Father,

I renounce _____, the lies I have thought about You.

I renounce _____, the lies I have thought about others.

I renounce _____, the lies I have thought about myself.

Repent

"If my people, who are called by my name, will humble themselves and pray and seek my face and turn from their wicked ways, then I will hear from heaven, and I will forgive their sin and will heal their land." *2 Chronicles 7:14.*

Father, forgive me for partnering with Satan and believing his lies about You.

Father, forgive me for partnering with Satan and believing his lies about others.

Father, forgive me for partnering with Satan and believing his lies about myself.

Pray

Father, give me the wisdom to not believe his lies and give me the strength to turn only to You for guidance in my life. You are the truth, the way, and the light. Amen

Rely On God's Mercy, Grace, and Power

"All the prophets testify about him that everyone who believes in him receives forgiveness of sins through his name." *Acts 10:41.*

Receive Forgiveness

Father, I receive your great forgiveness for my life. Because you have forgiven me, I can forgive myself.

Be Grateful

"Give thanks in every circumstance; for this is God's will for you in Christ Jesus." *1 Thessalonians 5:18.*

Father, I am grateful for Your love for me, even though I fall short.

Father, I am grateful for Your great love for me

Father, I am grateful that You are always there for me in times of trial and times of happiness.

Father, I am grateful that You guide and direct me as I love and serve others.

Amen.

Be Transformed

"Do not conform to the pattern of this world, but be transformed by the renewing of your mind. Then you will be able to test and approve what God's will is—his good, pleasing and perfect will." *Romans 12:2.*

"Whoever belongs to God hears what God says. The reason you do not hear is that you do not belong to God." *John 8:47.*

How Do We Meet Daily with God Through Prayer and Scripture?

Meeting God daily through the Bible and prayer is critically important for your Spiritual Life. It involves both listening to God's word and responding to Him in prayer. This provides a relationship of conversation and connection. It allows God to speak to you through the Bible. You can pause and reflect on His words, then respond with your own words, praising, thanking, and confessing to Him in prayer. To meet with God is not only to hear His words in the Bible. It is also to personally speak to Him directly in prayer.

It is a relationship with Him you are seeking. First, God speaks to you through the Bible. You listen carefully, as you take it all in. Many times, you speak to Him through your thoughts and feelings. This leads to responding to God with your own words of praise, thankfulness, confession, and prayer. God wants to hear back from you, so you can begin having a conversation with Him.

Prepare Your Heart

Dedicate a specific time and place daily just for God. This is a time to just focus on Him. You can do this in a variety of ways, such as sitting quietly listening to music, simply sitting still as you separate yourself from your daily life, and reading the Bible. Some people find their quiet space with God in nature, some in prayer, some in meditation, and some in music. No matter what the best way is for you, a regular time and place to meet with God is important.

Ask God to reveal Himself to you and help you hear His voice more clearly. Some people hear Him through the Bible, through music, through discernment, through dreams, and prayers. Whatever way is best for you is the right way. God is waiting to hear from you, no matter how you do it.

Speaking to God

It is not hard to speak to God. He is always there waiting for you to turn to Him. He has given you many ways to speak to Him. In prayer, you can pray using your own words or the prayers of others. With music, you can relax and wait for the conversation to start. In nature, you can take in His glory and listen for His voice. There are times you hear Him when you least expect Him. There are many other ways to talk with God. Any way you choose is the right way. God is always waiting for a conversation with you.

- Jesus emphasized talking to God directly and privately.
- Jesus taught the Lord's Prayer as a model, encouraging you to address God as Father, and to ask for your daily needs, forgiveness, and protection from temptation.
- Jesus emphasized the importance of praying in private, rather than for the sake of being seen by others. He stressed the importance of seeking God's will and not simply asking for what you want.
- Jesus taught that prayers should be offered in faith, believing that God will hear and answer.
- Jesus emphasized the reward of those who hear God's word and obey it.
- Jesus highlighted the importance of seeking God's will and the reward for you if you listen to and obey His word.

You can hear from God through His Word, through leading from the Holy Spirit, through prayer, and many other ways. If you are unaware, too distracted, or are just not being attentive to His voice, you can miss it. Remember, prayer is simply our conversation with God. A conversation is a two-way street. Hearing from God is sometimes understood as discerning His guidance and will in your life, not necessarily through audible voices. It is believed that God speaks to those who are seeking Him, living as per His teachings, praising Him, worshiping Him, thanking Him, and reaching out to Him when you need His help to overcome darkness. He is always present in your life, so there is no limit to the ways you can talk to Him and what the conversations will be about.

There are certainly times God reaches out to you, and sometimes you are not paying attention. It is important to think that talking to God is like talking to someone who truly wants the best for you and loves you deeply. It is important to remember that your faith in Him and willingness to follow His guidance allow you to build a strong and important communication with Him. Being humble and open to God's wisdom and the incorporation of all He has to say to you makes your life better. Hearing from God is a process of cultivating a relationship with Him, actively seeking His guidance, and listening to Him for guidance. He is always waiting to talk to us; we just need to listen and respond.

What Are Ways You Can Build a Relationship and Hear God's Voice?

Why Does God Sometimes Seem Silent?

"Whoever has ears, let them hear." *Matthew 11:15*. Because it is important, Jesus was encouraging you to pay attention to what He was saying. If you are too busy to listen to Him, you will miss what He is unfolding to you. Sometimes, even when you are pursuing Him, God seems silent. This could be because there are too many other things going on in your life. God needs your undivided attention if you want to hear His voice.

Too Many Other Voices Have Your Attention

God seems silent when too many other voices have your attention. If there is too much going on around you, it is hard to process anything. It is the same way when you are trying to hear Jesus. Too many other voices can distract you and cause you to miss what He is trying to tell you.

Questions

- Who are you going to for counsel?
- What advice are you reading or listening to on social media?
- Who are your closest friends?
- What music are you listening to?
- Who are your favorite influencers?
- Are the people and things in your life pulling you closer to Jesus, or are they pushing you further away from him?

You cannot effectively distinguish Jesus' voice from others when every other voice takes up a prominent place in your life. If you want to hear Jesus more clearly, start eliminating some of the voices that are not pointing to Him.

Are You Hungry Enough for God

Matthew 5:6. "Blessed are those who hunger and thirst for righteousness, for they shall be filled." God is always speaking, but if you cannot receive, you will not hear Him. If you are filled up with all the other voices, there is no room for you to process what God wants to say to you. If you want to hear God's voice, get hungry and empty your heart of everything else. Pursue God with your whole heart. If you are hungry for God, you will hear from Him.

Because God is always speaking and always available, you simply need a desire to hear His voice. Hearing Him is not difficult when you align your heart and mind with what He is saying. If you feel you have not heard from God in months or even years, here are some ways to start hearing Him again right away.

Reading His Word

The primary way to hear God's voice is by reading the Bible. If you are not spending time in His Word, it will be difficult to recognize His voice. "Man shall not live by bread alone, but by every word that comes from the mouth of God." *Matthew 4:4.*

Sermons are great, advice from friends is good, but God's word is the number one place for you to go for counsel. If you want to know God's heart, you must read His word. Reading the word can be daunting, especially if you are a beginner, but do not give up. The more you do it, the easier it is to talk to God and hear His responses.

Through Wise Counsel

God speaks to you through our leaders and the wise counsel of friends and family. King Saul disobeyed one of God's commandments by offering a sacrifice instead of the priest. Samuel, the prophet at the time, went to Saul and told him what he had done wrong. He also communicated God's punishment to Saul for his wrongful acts. *1 Samuel 13.*

Wise counsel is important because it helps you to stay on track and to get back on the right path when you stray. Saul needed someone like Samuel to correct him when he was doing wrong. Of course, make sure that the people who are offering you advice are trusted and that they draw their words of advice from God's word. 'Now the Philistines will come down against me at Gilgal, and I have not sought the favor of the Lord. So I forced myself, and offered the burnt offering." And Samuel said to Saul, "You have done foolishly. You have not kept the command of the Lord your God, with which he commanded you. For then the Lord would have established your kingdom over Israel forever." *Samuel 13:12-13.*

Pray

Prayer is simply a conversation between you and God. God often speaks to you through prayer and in quiet times. The issue is, sometimes your prayer tends to be one-sided. You tell God everything, but you do not leave room for Him to speak back. It is so important to take a few moments to simply sit in God's presence and hear what He is speaking from His heart to yours. Prayer is not just for you to pour out to God; it is also for you to receive from Him.

Worship Music

God can speak to us through music. The lyrics of worship music are often inspired by scripture. Sometimes, when God wants to communicate to you, He will use a song to get your attention. The entire book of Psalms is filled with poetry and songs. Do not be surprised if God uses the words of a song to speak to your heart.

Silence

God speaks through silence. You can hear God's voice the loudest as you sit with Him in silence. "I emptied myself of all the noise around me, I felt His presence more than ever before." *1 Kings 19:11-13a.* Sometimes you look for God in the loud and powerful. Perhaps God wants to pull you away from all of that and speak to you in the silence. It is easy to miss God when crowds of people surround you. It is much more difficult to miss Him in the silence when it is just you and Him. And He said, "Go out and stand on the mount before the Lord. And behold, the Lord passed by, and a great and strong wind tore the mountains and broke in pieces the rocks before the Lord, but the Lord was not in the wind. And after the wind an earthquake, but the Lord was not in the earthquake. And after the earthquake, a fire, but the Lord was not in the fire. And after the fire, the sound of a low whisper. And when Elijah heard it, he wrapped his face in his cloak and went out and stood at the entrance of the cave. And behold, there came a voice to him and said, "What are you doing here, Elijah?" *1 Kings 19:11-16.*

Nature

God can also speak to you through nature. Creation reveals who He is and allows you to experience His greatness. Nature is filled with beautiful metaphors. If you are truly listening, God can communicate through them. You can hear His voice while walking and taking in the beauty around you. If you are distracted by your phone or preoccupied with your to-do list, you may miss these moments, but even short walks or simply sitting in your own backyard can be meaningful. Take a moment to notice the beauty of nature and open your heart to whatever God may be saying to you. "When I look at Your heavens, the work of Your fingers, the moon and the stars, which you have set in place, what is man that you are mindful of Him and the Son of Man that you care for him?" *Psalms 8:3-4.*

Dreams

Today, dreams are overlooked in society. Maybe it is because you do not fully understand them, or because you do not realize that God still speaks through them today. God specifically tells you that in the last days, He will converse with His people through dreams. When you go to sleep tonight, ask God to speak to you through dreams. Ask Him to open your heart to understand what they mean. Write down your dreams once you wake up, pray about them, and search the Bible to find out what they could mean. "And it shall come to pass afterward, that I will pour out my Spirit on all flesh; your sons and your daughters shall prophesy, your old men shall dream dreams, and your young men shall see visions. Even on the male and female servants in those days, I will pour out my Spirit." *Joel 2:28-29.*

Remember, God is not limited in how He speaks. He can speak to you through many different means; these are only a few of them. Have ears to hear and a heart to receive, and you will always hear God's voice as He speaks into your life.

How Do Demons Respond When You Talk to God?

Demons are opposed to people praying to God. They see it as a direct threat to their efforts to hinder God's plan. They may try to interfere with your prayer by creating distractions or sowing doubts. However, God's power is greater. Prayer and conversations with God are powerful tools for overcoming demonic oppression.

- Demons use intimidation and oppression to threaten you.
- Demons use distraction and doubt during prayers, so that it makes it difficult for you to focus on prayers to God.
- Demons attempt to interfere with your prayers by creating distractions, sowing doubt, making you think that your prayer will not be answered, or that God is not listening.

When you pray, demons react with various forms of opposition. Though their direct response varies depending on the specific demon and context, some common responses include attempts to disrupt or distract you from prayer, to tempt you, and to instigate spiritual warfare. They look for any opportunity to gain influence over you. Demons often try to discourage prayer by projecting negative thoughts, feelings, or even causing physical disturbances.

How Demons Can Interfere Prayers

Disruption and Distraction

Demons try to make it difficult for you to focus on your prayers by projecting distracting thoughts, images, or even physical sensations.

Spiritual Warfare

Demons can engage in spiritual warfare by trying to manipulate or attack you through various means. As an example, they can send individuals who are under demonic influence to disrupt your prayers by telling you that praying does not do anything, God is not listening, or God does not care.

Seeking Openings

If you are already struggling with sin or open to demonic influence, demons will try to exploit where you are vulnerable, which increases the likelihood of further demonic activity.

Responding to Prayers Spoken Out Loud

Demons can respond to prayers, spoken aloud or said silently. They can hear and react to the words used. It is important to remember that the power of praying to God is stronger than any demon and that God is with you always. You do not need to be afraid of demons. Jesus's power and protection, along with the Holy Spirit, are enough to overcome anything. By focusing on Jesus and relying on the power of prayer, you will overcome the oppression of demons and remain steadfast in your faith.

Remember, demons are constantly working to separate you from God. Never believe those negative thoughts about God. God is and will always be there for you. God is always prepared to listen and guide you through life. God loves you more than you can ever understand and wants to be a part of your life. He loves us so much. He is always waiting to help you be who you are meant to be.

Family and Spiritual Warfare

What Is Spiritual Warfare for Your Family?

Satan knows that God created marriage as a beautiful, living picture of Christ and the Church. God designed both marriage and the family for your benefit. Satan knows the value of the family, how it is the very base of a good, solid society, a foundation of the Church, and the future of God's work on Earth. If Satan became successful in tearing down the structure and substance of the family unit, then he would be successful in damaging what is dear to God's heart.

Satan Attacks the Foundation of the Family – Marriage

When God finished creating the first couple, He called what He had made "very good." This man and woman were united in a holy bond before God. For the benefit of future generations, God explained, "Therefore a man shall leave his father and his mother and hold fast to his wife, and they shall become one flesh." *Genesis 2:24.* God requires a married couple a level of separation from others and a commitment to each other. This provides a stable foundation for the family unit.

Satan's initial attack on the family occurred in Eden, where the serpent worked his evil deception on Eve and destroyed the harmony of the first marriage. In listening to Satan and disobeying God, Eve and Adam, and all future generations were banished from the Garden. "So the Eternal God banished Adam and Eve from the Garden of Eden and exiled humanity from paradise, sentencing humans to laborious lives working the very ground man came from. After driving them out, He stationed winged guardians at the east end of the Garden of Eden and set up a sword of flames which alertly turned back and forth to guard the way to the tree of life. *Genesis 3:23-24.*

Due to the sin of Adam and Eve, all subsequent families inherited this judgment from God. Satan and his demons attack the family can be seen by all of us. With the increasing rate of divorce, the barrage of immorality, and the legalization of same gender marriages. There are signs of sin all around you. There are many, many influences in this world. You can see how successful Satan has been in twisting and perverting us, which can deny us the best God's meant for all families - the blessings of a holy marriage.

Satan's Attack on the Family Unit

Good marriages are the foundation of solid families. If Satan can successfully destroy the marriage, this will have a destructive impact on the rest of the family. It is believed that at least 85% of all children who exhibit behavioral disorders come from a fatherless home. Our society is shifting from a cohesive family to a marriage of cohabitation, which influences the stability of the home. Today, there is an increase in family instability.

The more closely you understand God's design for the family, the better you will be able to recognize when Satan tries to change and undermine it. Through Paul and Peter, God gives you clear instructions about the spheres of responsibility and authority within the family in *Ephesians 5:22-6:4*, *Ephesians 5:22*, *Ephesians 6:4*, *Colossians 3:18-21*, *1 Timothy 5:14*, *Titus 2:4-5*, and *1 Peter 3:1-7*. Two truths, which appear repeatedly in these passages, are the headship of the husband and the submission of the wife.

Scripture likens their relationship to that of Christ and the Church. It is expected that a husband maintain "Christ-like" leadership, assume the responsibility of protection and provision in the home. The husband is to love his wife and to give himself up to her, as Christ loves the Church. He is to nourish and cherish her. The wife is to submit to her husband, who is living out the responsibility God has given him. She has the divine calling of a wife and mother. This means to honor and affirm her husband's leadership and to help carry it through, according to her own gift from God. The husband is to love his wife "as Christ loved the Church and gave Himself up for her," and to "nourish and cherish" her as one would his own body. When the husband provides leadership marked by this sacrificial love, the wife will respect her husband, and the marriage will flourish. The husband, who is fulfilling his role as head, will seek to meet the needs of the family. The wife rests secure in the love and devotion of her husband and will support and help him in every possible way.

Satan has done an amazing job at distorting these two divine mandates from God - headship and submission. Often, you see men who authoritatively control families in a selfish, self-serving way. Also, you see which men give over the responsibility for guiding the family to the wife. While some women are dominated by their husbands, other women seek to be the controlling force in the home and do not respect their husbands. In these relationships, Satan has been very successful in persuading men and women to abandon God's plan.

When you believe that living out the principles of a Godly headship and submission is wrong, it will make your family life less than it should be. Satan has been successful in his evil work of deception. May God give today's husbands the courage to provide the loving leadership that God intended them to exercise, and wives the grace to respect and support their husbands.

The Scriptures provide clear guidelines for the children's place in family life. God instructs them to accept the authority of their parents, "Children, obey your parents in the Lord, for this is right. Honor your father. and mother" *Ephesians 6:1-2*. Satan and his demons are undermining the parental authority of the home, which introduces messages of disobedience. He seeks to render the parents unable to assert their authority over the children. Once you are aware of this truth, you can see the many specific ways that demons are doing today, in the media, literature, and music. Many television shows and children's books portray the father figure as weak or foolish. Numerous songs encourage children to resist parental authority. This is when demons are whispering to children that submission and obedience are not best for them. The music the children listen to, their entertainment, and the atmosphere of the home are important parental responsibilities. If fathers are to bring up children in the "discipline and instruction of the Lord," they must fulfill their leadership responsibilities in the family. This is to be done lovingly, without provoking their children to anger. *Ephesians 6:4*.

Satan's Attack on the Intention Of God For The Christian Home

The home is where the Word of God is taught and preserved, and where sound, Godly principle is explained and lived out. A godly life of faith, which characterized Timothy, was first shown in the home of his grandmother, then his mother, and then his own. From childhood, he was "acquainted with the sacred writings" which were able to make him "wise unto salvation through faith in Christ Jesus." *2 Timothy 3:15.* You must let the Bible be a priority in the home, because God's Word is the necessary foundation. Satan has done a fantastic job of keeping your family so busy that you barely have time to read the Bible, let alone study it and apply it to your life. Spending time in God's Word and waiting upon God is essential. If Satan can keep you and your family too busy for the Bible, you can lose your joy, strength, and effectiveness in this world. Satan uses busyness as a tool to rob your family of the time God wants you to spend together. As a result, you miss out on closeness and the enjoyment of each other's company.

Husbands and wives need time together to nurture their relationship. They need time with their children, if they are going to fulfill the Biblical mandate of training up a child in the way he should go, *Proverbs 22:6*. Training your children requires your time and attention. But when you become frantically busy or overwhelmed, it is easy to lose focus and miss those meaningful moments with them. Your family needs intentional time, when the earplugs are out, the Internet is shut down, the phone is silenced, and everyone's needs are met with love and care.

Take time to read and pray together, to eat and play together. As you live out God's plan for your family, He will be glorified, and your home will be richly blessed.

When you spend time with God and allow your behavior to be guided by God's Word, this will produce Christlike thinking and behavior in you, which will draw your children's hearts to God. Any way in which Satan can keep you and your children's lives from exhibiting the fruit of the Spirit (love, joy, peace, patience, kindness, goodness, faithfulness, gentleness, self-control), your family's character will be weakened, and everyone will suffer loss. When he can plant the seed of unforgiveness, the peace and joy of your family are destroyed. If he can convince your family members to act hypocritically, integrity is lost. If he can persuade your children or you to stretch the truth or shade it, even the smallest bit, trust is destroyed, and damage follows. Your family's ultimate protection against Satan's attacks is to know and live out God's truth. As His truth and love are expressed through the functioning of your family, even neighbors and friends may be drawn to God.

Ways To Fight Back for Your Family

Be A Prayer Warrior

When you do not pray until there is a problem. When you do pray for your children, it is usually for their safety, and while that is important, remember that Satan and his demons target their minds first. The way your children think shapes the decisions they make. That is why you need to be a prayer warrior for your family.

You need to identify specific things you pray for each of your children- things that are godly and come straight from the Bible. Do not pray that your son wins the ballgame. Instead, pray that he displays a godly attitude, whether he wins or loses. Pray these things with your children so they understand what is most important to God.

- If you have school-age children, pray regularly for their teachers and administrators. Pray that school is a spiritual battleground. Instead of being scared about what your children are facing each day, be active in it through prayer.
- Go ask the principal, "How can I pray for you and your staff?".
- Ask your child's teacher, "How can I be praying over your classroom today?" And if they do not have an answer, be ready to tell them what you are praying for them, specifically.

Start praying now for godly friends for your children. Do not forget to pray for your marriage daily. Demons want to disrupt your home. If they cannot destroy your family, they will settle for anger and conflict. Satan does not want your children to grow up with godly parents. So, pray Scripture over your spouse, just as you do for your kids. For your prayers to be effective, you have to recognize your sins, confess them, and repent of them. We may even need to apologize to your children for something they have heard you say or seen you do that does not reflect Christ.

Be A Teacher

Being a parent, it is a part of your responsibility to teach your children what is true and what is not based on the Word of God. It is not just about keeping evil out; it is about putting righteousness in. God answers all your questions about all that is facing you and what your children are facing in this culture. The Bible tells you and your children how to respond, what attitudes to have and not have, and how to find strength and comfort on your and their most difficult days.

But you have to be active in that. You, as their parent, are their primary teacher. If you feel you do not know enough about the Bible, there is an easy answer: Just read it. You do not have to know all the answers; you just have to be willing to learn.

Be An Example

Children learn about God by watching you. You can send them to a Christian school, but they will get confused if they do not see what they learned in school lived out at home. That means you have to make a wholehearted commitment to Christ. It is obedience to God without compromise. It is refusing to tolerate or participate in anything God calls evil, including your entertainment choices.

Be an Obstacle

There is no doubt that there is a spiritual war going on for your family and my family. But you can be an obstacle in Satan's way. You can decide to be more enthusiastic about your children and grandchildren, like knowing about the games and instruments they play.

Be a Prayer Warrior

Pray for them daily as examples:

"Lord, I want to be more passionate than my children to know You and grow in You, than I am about anything else."

"Lord, I yearn for my children to be protected from all harm. Holy Spirit, watch over them and guide them through their day."

Your children deserve their mothers and fathers to be there for them. Demons should have to crawl over the godly parents and grandparents. Also, be a prayer warrior in your church family. Help other families as they pray for their children. We all need to take a stand for righteousness. If demons are coming to steal, kill, and destroy my children and grandchildren, they have to come against me first!

God, who created the family, has provided the divine design and instruction in His Word so that you and your family can flourish. Our best defense is to know the pattern, so that you will be able to discern Satan's subtle attacks, and to let the fruit of the Spirit characterize your life. You need godly leadership, respect, and love, along with enthusiastic prayer and dependence on God. He alone can preserve your family. He loves you and wants the best for all of you.

"Dear Lord, Help families to follow His truth and cling closely to Him." Amen.

How Can You Pray for Protection Over Yourself and Your Family?

To Be Read Aloud:

Heavenly Father,

I bow in worship and praise before You. I cover myself with the blood of the Lord Jesus Christ as my protection. I surrender myself completely in every area of my life to You. I take a stand against all the workings of Satan that would hinder me in my prayer life. You are the only True and Living God. I refuse any involvement of Satan in my life and prayers. I command Satan, in the Name of the Lord Jesus Christ, to leave my presence with all of his demons. Holy Spirit, bring the blood of the Lord Jesus Christ between Satan and my family. Amen

Heavenly Father,

I worship You and give You praise. I recognize that You are worthy to receive all glory and honor and praise. I renew my commitment to You and pray that the Holy Spirit will enable me during this time of prayer. I am thankful, Heavenly Father, that You have loved me from the beginning and that You sent the Lord Jesus Christ into the world to die for my sins. I am thankful that Jesus came as my Savior and that through Him I am completely forgiven. You have adopted me into Your family; You have assumed all responsibility for me. You have given me eternal life. I am thankful that through Jesus, You have made me complete, and that You have offered Yourself to me and my family to be my daily help and strength. Amen

Heavenly Father,

Open my eyes that I might see how great You are and how complete Your provision is for this day. I am thankful for the victory Jesus Christ won for me on the Cross. In His Resurrection, faith and salvation have been given to me. I am thankful I am a child of God. I take my place as God's child. Through my faith, baptism, and the presence of the Holy Spirit, I declare that Satan and his demons have no hold on me and are subject to our Lord Jesus Christ. I am thankful for the Armor You have provided. I put on the Belt of Truth, the Breastplate of Righteousness, the Shoes of Peace, and the Helmet of Salvation. I lift up the Shield of Faith against all evil. I take in my hand the Sword of the Spirit, the Word of God. I choose to use Your Word against all the forces of evil in my life. I put on this Armor and live and pray in complete dependence upon You. I am grateful, Heavenly Father, that Jesus Christ triumphed over all demonic principalities and powers. I claim all that victory for my life today. I reject all the insinuations, accusations, lies, and temptations of Satan. I affirm that the Word of God is true, and I choose to live today in the light of God's Word. I choose to live in obedience to You, Father. I choose to worship You as my loving, almighty God. Open my eyes and show me the areas of my life that do not please You. Work in me to cleanse me from all sin that would give Satan a foothold against me. I do stand as Your adopted child, and I welcome all the ministry of the Holy Spirit. By faith and dependence upon You, I stand in all the victory of the Resurrection and the provision Jesus Christ has given me to live above sin. Therefore, today I take off the sinful nature with its selfishness and pride. I put on the new nature with its love. I take off the old nature with its fear, and I put on the new nature with its courage. I take off the old nature with its weakness, and I put on the new nature with its strength. I take off the old nature with all its deceitful lusts, and I put on the new nature with its righteousness, purity, and honesty. In every way, I stand in the victory of the Death, Burial, and Resurrection of my Lord Jesus Christ. I claim my place in Christ as victorious with Him over all the enemies of my soul. Holy Spirit, I pray that You would fill me. Come into my life, break down every idol and cast out every demon, and guide and direct me in the ways of God. Amen

Heavenly Father,

I am thankful for the expression of Your will in my daily life. As You have shown me in Your Word, I claim the will of God for me today. I am thankful that You have blessed me with all spiritual blessings through Christ Jesus. I am thankful that You have made me a living hope by the resurrection of

Jesus Christ from the dead. I am thankful that You have provided for me today, so I can live filled with the Spirit of God, with love, joy and peace, long suffering, gentleness and goodness, meekness, faithfulness, and self-control in my life. I recognize that this is Your will for me, and I reject and resist all the endeavors of Satan and his demons to rob me of the will of God. I refuse i to believe my feelings. I hold up the shield of faith against all the accusations, distortions, insinuations and lies that Satan would put into my mind. I claim the will of God for my life today. In the Name of the Lord Jesus Christ, I completely surrender myself to You, Heavenly Father, as a living sacrifice. I choose not to conform to this world. I choose to be transformed by the renewing of my mind, and I pray that You would show me Your will and enable me to walk in all the fullness of Your will today. Amen.

Heavenly Father,

I am thankful that the weapons of our warfare are mighty through God, to pull down strongholds, to cast down every high thing that exalts above God, and to bring every thought into obedience to the Lord Jesus Christ. Therefore, in my own life today, I tear down the strongholds of Satan and smash the plans of Satan that have been formed against me. I tear down the strongholds of Satan against my mind, my emotions, and my body, and I surrender them all to You. I affirm, Heavenly Father, that You have not given me the spirit of fear but of power and love and a sound mind. I break and smash the strongholds of Satan formed against my emotions today, and I give my emotions to You. I smash the strongholds of Satan formed against my mind today, I give my will to You, and choose to make the right decisions of faith. I smash the strongholds of Satan formed against my body today. I give my body to You, recognizing that I am Your temple. I rejoice in Your mercy and goodness. Amen.

Heavenly Father,

I pray that this day You will strengthen and enlighten me. Show me the way Satan is hindering, tempting, lying, and distorting the truth in my life. Enable me to be the kind of person that would please You. Enable me to be active in prayer and faith. Enable me to mentally think about and practice

Your Word, and to give You Your rightful place in my life. I cover myself with the blood of the Lord Jesus Christ and pray that You, Holy Spirit, will bring guidance, courage, and strength into my life. I give myself to You. I refuse to be discouraged. You are the God of all hope, and I claim victory over all of Satan's forces in my life. I pray in the Name of the Lord Jesus Christ with thanksgiving. Amen.

How Do I Cleanse My Home and Property of Demonic Influence?

As a believer in Christ and through the power of the Holy Spirit, you have authority over demons. By following the steps of prayer, anointing, and cleansing, you can ensure your home becomes and remains a peaceful, holy space where the presence of God lives. Be diligent in spiritual house cleaning, anointing, and prayers. You can trust God will protect and bless your home when you stay diligent in spiritual house cleaning.

Spiritual house cleansing, as understood through the Bible, involves prayer, seeking God's protection, and potentially, casting out demons. Biblical passages that relate to Spiritual House Cleansing are found In *Matthew 12:43-45*, *Luke 11:24*, and *Psalm 91*.

Ways To Tell If There Is a Demonic Influence in Your Home

- You have no peace in your home. Everyone is fighting and at odds with each other.
- You discern that something is not right.
- Someone returned from a trip and unknowingly brought back a demonic object.
- Pornography in the home.
- Spiritual attacks at home.
- After watching something on TV or any other kind of media, one can feel a disturbing presence.
- When visitors enter or leave your home and the atmosphere negatively changes.
- A person in the home is practicing witchcraft, Santeria, or any other pagan religion.
- A family member is in emotional bondage.

Remove Entertainment That Pollutes Your Home

Watch what you allow in your home under the guise of entertainment. Some people may say, "It's just a movie." Or "It's only TV, we all know it is not real." Young children cannot discern if it is real or not. It is not just entertainment. TV programming programs our minds. Entertainment can be very, very wicked. Would you allow someone to come into your house and blaspheme the name of the Lord, as entertainment does? You cannot un-see the evil once you have taken it in with your eyes and ears. Use discernment with entertainment, as well as all the objects permitted in your home.

Look for any non-Christian items, both inside and outside of your home, which are related to the occult or Satan, such as art, books, magazines, music, movies, décor, jewelry, clothing, etc. These items are considered to be "Open Doors", which are ways Satan and his demons can enter or re-enter your life and your home. If you find anything, you must destroy it immediately—either by burning it or by wrapping it up and throwing it away.

If anything that is of the demonic or darkness and does not bring light into your home, it needs to be removed from your home. These are all open doors and provide a way for Demons to get in. To protect yourself and your family, you can follow these actions.

Blessed Oil or Water for Spiritual Protection

Use blessed oil or water to anoint each room in your house. Blessed oil and water involve seeking God's power and presence in these elements. Blessed oil and water have long been used in healing, protection, and spiritual cleansing.

Prayer For Blessing Oil

"Father, I humbly come before you to ask for your blessing upon this oil. I ask that you fill it with Your divine power and presence, that it may be a conduit of Your grace and protection. I dedicate this oil for protection and spiritual strengthening. I pray that wherever it is used, it will bring forth your blessings. May it be a source of strength and protection for those who are in need. I ask this in the name of our Lord and Savior, Jesus Christ." Amen.

Prayer for Blessing Water

"Father, I humbly come before you to ask for your blessing upon this water. I ask that you fill it with Your divine power and presence, that it may be a conduit of Your grace and protection. I dedicate this water for protection and spiritual strengthening. I pray that wherever it is used, it will bring forth your blessings. May this water be a source of strength and protection for this family, and may it be a reminder of your grace and love. I ask this in the name of our Lord and Savior, Jesus Christ." Amen.

House Blessing

House Blessing can be done individually or with your family and friends. Walking through each room, family member(s) place the sign of the cross over the windows and internal doors in the room with oil or water. Each time you make the sign of the Cross over the external doorways you can pray one or more of these prayers.

- "Come, Holy Spirit. Come and fill every part of this home with the fullness of the kingdom of God, with your love, your peace, and your rest. May Your Holy Spirit flow through and fill this home up with Your Spirit." Amen
- "Lord, bless me, my family, and friends coming through this door. Lord bless delivery persons doing their jobs, any strangers, rich or poor. Help me welcome everyone and pass along Your peace, and whether I'm coming or going, may my love for you increase". Amen
- "Let us now pray that the Holy Spirit will enter this home and bless it with His presence. May He always be here among us; may He nurture our love for each other, share in our joys, and comfort us in our sorrows. We pray this in the name of Jesus, our Lord."

House Cleansing Prayers

A Christian house cleansing prayer can be a powerful way to spiritually bless your home. This house cleaning prayer can be repeated, if needed. As you pray, consider walking through each room, specifically asking for cleansing and protection in those areas. While praying out loud, you can use anointing oil or blessed water to draw a cross on the doors and windows. This symbolizes the protection of God, as demonstrated at the time of Moses. Personalize the prayer, if you like. Do not use sage or any other substance, symbol, or device that is used in non-Christian rites. Incorporate scripture readings into your cleansing prayers.

Command any lingering demonic spirits to leave in Jesus' name. Pay close attention to rooms where you have sensed conflict, discomfort, or spiritual heaviness. Use prayers that focus on rebuking evil and inviting God's presence into your home. Declare that your home is a place for the Holy Spirit to dwell.

A Christian house cleansing prayer can be a powerful way to spiritually cleanse and bless your home. This house cleaning prayer can be repeated if needed.

- "In the name of Jesus Christ, I command any demon to leave this space and take any negativity, darkness, or unholy influences with you. I invite the Holy Spirit to fill this home with your presence, love, and peace. I dedicate this house to You, Lord, and ask that it be a place of joy, healing, and blessing. I thank you for your faithfulness and protection. Amen"
- "Jesus, I ask that you would also send your angels to cleanse this home now, to establish your kingdom here, and to build a shield of protection around it. Please guard all who enter and leave. Let nothing enter this house that is not of you. Amen."

Prayers of Protection

- "Heavenly Father, I come before you today, seeking Your guidance and protection for this home. I ask that you cleanse this space of any negativity, darkness, or unholy influences. I command any evil spirits or forces to leave this home in the name of Jesus. I invite your Holy Spirit to fill this home with your presence, love, and peace. I dedicate this house to you, Lord, and ask that it be a place of joy, healing, and blessing. I thank you for your faithfulness and protection. Amen."
- "Lord Jesus, You are the Head of my household. I invite Your authority and dominion to reign over this place. Through the name power of Your name, I bind every demon and cast them into the abyss. Through the name of Jesus Christ, I command that no demonic forces are permitted to operate or linger here. Amen."
- "Heavenly Father, I come before you asking your presence and protection in this home. I ask that you cleanse this space of evil influences or spiritual disturbances. May Your holy light shine brightly in every corner of every room, filling it with Your love and peace. I pray that You surround this home and all who dwell within it with your divine protection. Guard us from all harm, both seen and unseen, and keep us safe from any spiritual attacks. I ask that you bless this home and all who enter it, that they may feel Your presence and experience Your peace. In the name of Jesus Christ, I command all demons to leave this home. Thank you, Jesus, for cleansing and purifying this home. Thank you, Lord, for your constant presence and protection. Through the protection of the Holy Spirit and Your angels, may this home be a sanctuary of peace, love, and joy, where Your name is honored and Your will be done. Amen."

Property Cleansing

It is important to remember that many properties have been lived on and houses lived in by others. Some demonic interference within a home can be caused by demons living there before you moved in. This can also include demons outside. Demonic interference may not be caused by your actions, but by the actions of others. For that very reason now is the time pray for the removal of any demonic force from your yard.

Removal of Demon Interference on Your Property

- Clear the Area

Remove any trash, debris, or items that could be harboring demonic forces like pagan symbols, statuary, unknown objects, or clutter.

- Clean the Yard

Sweep, mow, or weed the lawn to create a sense of order and clarity.

- Clean Surfaces

Wash or scrub any surfaces in the yard, including patios, decks, or furniture

Pray Protection

To pray for the protection of your yard from demons, focus on seeking God's power and presence, invoking angels, and rebuking evil influences. You can use specific prayers, like the one from Exodus 90, which asks for a perimeter of protection around you and your loved ones, including the yard. You can also use Psalm 91, which speaks of God's refuge and protection.

Renounce

- "I renounce and ask that You forgive the sins that have defiled this land by anyone at any time, especially the sins of Satanism, Witchcraft, idolatry, bloodshed, immorality, and breaking of covenants made to You. Amen"
- "I renounce all ungodliness and all sinful activity that has ever taken place in this home or on this land. I renounce the

sin of all previous owners, renters, guests, and builders. Any curses or evil agreements ever made in or over this home, I now declare broken, null, and void in the name and authority of Jesus. In the name of Jesus, I also command every demon to be bind together now and to leave my home. I cancel every claim and right the enemy might have here, by the blood of Jesus Christ. Please cleanse this home and everything in it with the blood of Christ. Amen"

Request Protection

- "Lord Jesus, in Your love and mercy to establish a perimeter of protection around my family, myself, and all our loved ones. I ask that the Holy Angels guard us and all our possessions, and this property, rendering us immune from any kind of demonic influence. I ask that no demonic bondage, door, demonic entity, portal, astral projection, or disembodied spirit may enter the property in any direction. I ask You to send us your Angels to protect us from harm, including any demon interference or involvement within the vicinity of our property. I ask that, should demons try to enter, they be prevented by your Angels. That You will strip them of all weapons and authority. That You will bind, rebuke, and disable them from communicating or interacting with each other or with us. Please remove them, sending them directly to the Abyss. All this I ask in Your Holy Name. Amen"

Binding Demons

- "Lord Jesus, in your Holy Name, I ask you to bind up any demonic forces from manifesting on our property. In Your Holy Name, I ask you to remove any demons or demon attachments from our property. Amen"
- "In Jesus' name, I bind all spirits in the air, and the fire and the water, in the ground and the underground. I bind any

satanic forces of nature," I command any unclean thing that is not of you to leave immediately in Jesus' name. Amen"
- "Lord Jesus, I ask You to render all spirits impotent, paralyzed, and ineffective in attempting to take revenge against me, my family, my friends, my community, and those who pray for me and my family. I ask You to bind all evil spirits, all powers of the air, the water, the ground, the fire, underground, or wherever they exercise their powers, any satanic forces in nature, and any emissaries of the satanic headquarters. I ask You to bind, by Your Precious Blood, all of the attributes, aspects, and characteristics, interactions, communications, and deceitful games of demons. I ask You to break any and all bonds, ties, and attachments. Amen."

Consecrate Your Home to God

Consecrating your Home to God involves setting it apart for a sacred purpose through prayer and dedication, and often a specific ceremony. This can involve a prayer, declaring the land as belonging to God, and making a commitment to using it in a way that honors Him.

"Father, I now consecrate and dedicate this home and the land it is on to the rule of Jesus, the presence of the Holy Spirit, and the Kingdom of God. I dedicate everything in and around this house to the Lord Jesus and claim that it is under His rule, protection, and blessing – every room, all the appliances, the structure and infrastructure, the water, and the electricity. Come, Holy Spirit. Come and fill every part of this home with the fullness of the kingdom of God, with your love, your peace, and your rest. Jesus, I ask that You would also send Your angels to cleanse this home now, to establish Your kingdom here, and to build a shield of protection around it. In the mighty name of The Lord Jesus Christ, I now proclaim that this home, land, and everything in it is property of the Kingdom of God. Amen"

Ongoing Prayers

- "Lord, I invite Your authority and dominion to reign over this place. Through the power of Your name, I bind every spiritual enemy and cast them far from these premises. I command that no demonic forces are permitted to operate or linger here. Establish Your kingdom rule, and let angelic guards surround and protect this home."
- "Come, Holy Spirit. Come and fill every part of this home with the fullness of the kingdom of God, with your love, your peace, and your rest. Jesus, I ask that you would also send your angels to cleanse this home now, to establish your kingdom here, and to build a shield of protection around it. In the mighty name of Jesus Christ the Lord, I now proclaim that his home, land, and everything in it is property of the Kingdom of God."

Demons and Spiritual Warfare

What Are Open Doors?

How Do Demons Gain Access To People's Lives?

God sees the human body as a dwelling place. Scripture calls the body of the believer the temple of the Holy Spirit. *1 Corinthians 6:19.* But Satan and his demons also see the human body as a place to live. *Matthew 12:43-45.* "When an unclean spirit goes out of a man, he goes through dry places, seeking rest, and finds none. Then he says, 'I will return to my house from which I came.' And when he comes, he finds it empty, swept, and put in order. Then he goes and takes with him seven other spirits more wicked than himself, and they enter and dwell there; and the last state of that man is worse than the first." The demon in this passage referred to the man as his house. Demons crave bodies to inhabit and express their nature through. Without such a body, they are restless because they have no home. But a demon cannot simply enter into any person that they choose; there must be an open door in the house for it to have entrance. Several things can open the door for demonic access into your life. These open doors give demons a place to enter and dwell within you.

Descriptions Of Some Open Doors

Ongoing Sin

When you fail to confess and repent of sin, you come into agreement with Satan, and this gives him the right to an area of your life. Blatant rebellious sin or ongoing hidden sin can be a demonic entry point. Paul warns that if we do not properly deal with anger, it will provide a place for demons to enter. "In your anger do not sin, do not let the sun go down while you are still angry, and do not give the devil a foothold." *Ephesians 4:26-27.* If you find yourself unable to break free from a persistent sinful habit, it is possible that an evil spiritual is influencing your life. In such cases, the demon must be driven out through the Deliverance Ministry to experience true freedom.

Traumatic Experiences

When you go through a traumatic experience, many times a demon can gain access to your life. Being sinned against or exploited can open a door for demons. For example, being abused sexually, physically, or verbally can give a demon entry into your life, causing you to be tormented by that traumatic experience. Then you feel only hate, pain, and agony. These feelings can cause you to turn away from God. It seems unfair that a person can become demonized through another person's action, but Satan does not play fair. Various types of traumatic events and all types of abuse can open the door to demonic oppression.

Believing Demons

Satan is called the father of lies. His demons know no other language but lies. When you believe in his lies, you agree with him. His goal is to steal, kill, and destroy you in any way he can, as he works on taking souls from God. When you believe a lie about God or yourself, you open the way for a lying demon to reinforce that lie in your life.

Exposure To Unholy Things

Being exposed to unholy things can open the door to demons. Some examples are books, pornography, horror movies, dark music, occult items or idols, Eight Ball, Pokémon, Dungeons and Dragons, Fortune Telling, Astrology, Symbols of Witchcraft, Satanism, Masons, Eastern Star, any representation of the Devil, Demons, pagan gods or goddesses in jewelry, art books, non-Biblical Religions Yoga, Hinduism, Witchcraft, Satanism, Ancient Religions practices including art, books, music, jewelry. There are many more. There is a reason why God commands His people to come out from among the world and be holy.

Withholding Forgiveness

Having bitterness, resentment, or unforgiveness toward others is an open door for evil spirits. The parable of the unmerciful servant, *Matthew 18:15-35,* shows that at the end of the parable, the unforgiving servant is put into prison to be tormented. Withholding forgiveness from others puts you into a spiritual prison and gives the devil permission to torment you; this is a serious issue and a major root cause for many other problems. You must learn to forgive the ones who have hurt you. This is done through the same grace that Christ gave to all of us through His Crucifixion. You can pray wellness over them and walk through the process of releasing them to the Lord. This does not mean that what they did was okay, and it does not mean that you cannot maintain boundaries with those who hurt you. But you must choose to walk in forgiveness as God has forgiven you.

Involvement in False Religion, Cults, and False Teaching

Behind every idol is a demon *1 Corinthians 10:19-20* and false teaching carries with it a false spirit *Corinthians 11:4* and *1 Timothy 4:1*. It makes sense that those who become involved with cults and who believe false teachings can become demonized. Whether it is blatant false teaching like Buddhism, Hinduism, and the worship of idols, gods, Satan, or even the use of subtle erroneous teachings within the church. All of these can open a door for a demon to enter.

Any Occult Involvement

Contact with the occult is a major open door to the demonic and is strictly forbidden in Scripture, *Deuteronomy 18:9-12*. There are two sources of supernatural power in the world: God and Satan. The word occult means "secret or hidden" and refers to the supernatural realm of Satan. Some examples include Witchcraft, fortunetelling, communication with the dead, magic arts, eastern meditation, sorcery, Ouija board, astrology, Satanism, new age teachings, psychics, astral projection, and channeling. This is not an all-inclusive list, but it should give you an idea of what to avoid. If you had any contact with the occult, even if it was a long time ago and it was just for fun, I encourage you to verbally renounce your involvement and seek Deliverance Ministry.

Curses

Another open door is the area of curses. While the idea of curses is often dismissed as mere superstition in the West, it appears frequently throughout the Bible. What is referred to as generational curses could certainly be an open door. This is when either sinful actions or negative attributes get passed down through a generational line. Another type of curse is what is called a word curse.

James 3:8-10 talks about the tongue and how blessing and cursing can proceed from the same mouth, and *Proverbs 18:21* says that death and life are in the power of the tongue. Some parents do not realize that they are literally cursing their children by saying things like "you are so stupid" or "you will never amount to anything." These open doors are not meant to be an exhaustive list; much more could be said about each one. The key point is this: doors can often be opened in your life without your awareness. When you cast out demons, it is crucial to identify the root causes of the problem and ensure that every door is closed. Once a door has been closed, it is your responsibility, with the help of the Holy Spirit, to keep it that way.

What Are Demons' Legal Rights?

The process of deliverance often consists of three main parts: Tearing down strongholds, removing legal rights, and then casting out the remaining demons. If you try to cast out demons without taking away the strongholds or legal rights that they are holding onto, you may not be successful. Removing all of these is vital in going for a complete and successful Deliverance.

What Are Legal Rights?

A legal right is something that can allow demons to enter or harass you, or give them the right to remain in you, even when you try to cast them out. Some of the most common legal rights that are faced when ministering deliverance are:

Sins

When you sin, it gives the enemy a legal right to affect or bother you in one way or another. When you allow unholy thoughts to enter your mind, it opens the door to a demon. Eventually, this causes you to commit more sins. It all starts when the enemy tempts you to observe the wrong thing. When you accept your sins and you make it a habit, a new door is opened, so more demons can move in further behind the bad habit. If you continue down this path, more doors are opened to Satan and his demons. Eventually, you will find yourselves sinning by lying, stealing, committing adultery, rape, and more. The feelings and desires demons push on you are irresistible. Once these sins are committed, more doors are opened. This problem is like a snowball rolling down a hill. Sin opens the door to demons, which pushes you in the direction of committing more sins, which causes you to open more doors.

The answer is repentance. You need to verbally confess and repent of the sins that have given Satan legal rights in your life. If you recognize a particular sin or sins that have opened the doors to the bondage you are experiencing and from which you seek deliverance, repent sincerely of those sins that caused the bondage.

Any larger or gross sins you can remember, it is always good to repent of them specifically. Repentance is very important to Deliverance. *1 John 1:9* tells you to confess your sins. If you do not confess your sins and try to hide them from others, and if you do not repent of these sins to Jesus, it leaves that sin in your life, causing havoc and pain. We have to confess our sins to God to be forgiven.

Some Types of Sins

Soul Ties

Repentance, renunciation, and breaking of soul ties are important. First, specifically repent of the sin that caused the soul tie to be formed in the first place. Then use your authority through Jesus Christ to break and sever the unholy soul tie. Again, repentance and the breaking of the soul ties in Jesus' name are the way to go about solving this problem.

Demonic Oaths and Vows

A demonic vow can be like a spiritual signature that demons use as a legal right to gain access to your life. Demonic vows can be made consciously or unconsciously. Often, if you join a cult, a Satanist, a Coven, or even some organizations, you may be required to make vows to Satan, which you may not realize you are doing. This gives the demon legal right to be in your life. Demonic vows can be made unconsciously just by dabbling with the occult, even just being curious about the occult, and reading forbidden materials, which include horoscopes, telling demons that you are interested in them. The only vows that are practical and good are those made in the name of Jesus, such as weddings, Baptism, Vows to God, etc. If you have made vows that do not glorify God, then you should repent and renounce those vows verbally and seek God's forgiveness.

Unforgiveness

When you do not forgive others, God does not forgive you. When God does not forgive you, it leaves your sins remaining, which can give demons legal rights in your life. *Matthew 18:21-35*, the Parable of the Unforgiving Servant. Keep in mind that the tormentors are referring to demons. The legal ground the enemy may be standing on to torment you may very well be rooted in unforgiveness. Forgiveness is not an option; it is a necessity. It is the key to your relationship with God. So, repent for holding bitterness in your heart against others and make a solid choice to forgive those who have wronged you. Confirm your choice of forgiveness by verbally forgiving others. This releases the bitterness and hurt from your heart against others. Forgiveness is an act of Grace, just as God forgave us through Jesus Christ.

Generational Curses

Generational Curses can produce negative traits and behavior, especially dysfunctional behaviors. Misfortunes can be passed down through a family's bloodlines from one generation to the next. They are rooted in sin or trauma. The experiences of your ancestors can create a negative legacy and impact subsequent generations. These cures are not necessarily your fault. Breaking Generational Curses will break these curses for your children and future generations. Generational Curses can often be seen passed down family bloodlines through addiction, adultery, physical and emotional abuse, lack of faith in God, and other sins. Generational Curses are very common.

Childhood Rejection

Much demonic bondage is caused during childhood. For example, if you were rejected as a child, a demon of rejection can enter. If you have been rejected by either your parents or anyone else. The demon of rejection is usually present in these situations and should be cast out. To completely overcome this rejection, you must make a solid choice to forgive that person(s), and release the hurt in your heart against them to God.

Points of Weakness

When the person experiences weakness, such as emotional shock, physical trauma, fearful experiences during childhood, and other areas. The natural wall of defense in the physical, spiritual, or emotional system of a person is weakened. It leaves you vulnerable for the enemy to attach himself to you. The same is true with drinking excessive amounts of alcohol and using drugs. The reason is that drugs and alcohol lower our defenses. Since demons thrive on weakness, they love to move right in and begin to deceive you, so they can pull you farther away from God.

The Remedy

If there is any bitterness involved (say somebody caused the traumatic experience for you, and you are still holding it against them), then you must forgive the person who hurt you, and repent for holding onto the bitterness in your heart towards them. If the point of weakness was caused by your own sin, such as drinking or drugs, then confess and repent of those sins. If the demons entered solely through a traumatic experience, and it was your fault, then the demons have a Stronghold on your mind, body, and emotions in this situation. They need to be cast out.

Spoken Self-Curses

The words we say have spiritual value; the Bible says to bless and not curse, and that the tongue has the power of life and death. If you walk around saying, "I wish I could just die," a demon may hear you and then push you closer to death through the power of his lies. If this is the case, renounce what you said or thought against yourself. Then, as a child of God, repent for thinking and speaking such things. Ask God for forgiveness, and then you forgive yourself. Say, "In the name of Jesus Christ, I break all curses I have spoken against myself, and I put it under the blood of Jesus." You can repeat this as many times as you need.

Cursed Objects

Physical objects can carry spiritual value, such as idols, occult books, rings, movies, charms, etc. If you brought any Indian or pagan religious artifacts into your home, you could be opening the door for demons to enter and oppress the people within your home. Land can also become defiled by the sins of its owners, *Leviticus 18:27*. Burn, destroy, or get rid of any physical objects that you have located that could be cursed or of Satan. *Isaiah 2:18*, "And the idols he shall utterly abolish." It is Biblical to burn cursed objects. If you are responsible for bringing such objects into your home, repent. Land can be cleansed by prayer and repentance for the sins of the previous owners.

Renounce Demons

Renounce any known demons that have been invited through spirit guides, seances, demonic rituals, and any interest or involvement in the occult - Witchcraft, Satanism, etc. Also, renounce any demons that you know need to be cast out. This explains to the demons that you are no longer interested in having them around, and you are taking measures to cast them out.

Other Helpful Things to Look For

When did the bondage start? Try to identify how the problem started and what gave the demons the ability to enter. Look for any involvement in the occult, sins, vows, traumatic experiences, etc., along with any unusual happenings - emotional, mental, or physical.

What Are Demonic Soul Ties?

Soul ties refer to the process of breaking unhealthy emotional and spiritual bonds with others that are mainly based on ungodly principles or relationships. This involves identifying, confessing, repenting, and, through Jesus Christ, breaking these connections. You need to break all negative or sinful Soul Ties to achieve total freedom.

What are Soul Ties?

Soul ties can form through various interactions, including romantic relationships, close friendships, prolonged interactions at work, family connections, vows and agreements, trauma and abuse, and spiritual practices. They can be positive, building healthy bonds with others. Or they can be negative, hindering spiritual growth and creating unhealthy dependencies. Un-godly soul ties, in particular, are those that are built on sin, such as co-dependency, harmful attachments, or a lack of boundaries. Soul ties can lead to emotional, spiritual, or even physical harm.

Soul ties can be formed through:

Unhealthy Emotional Dependence:

Feeling anxious when separated from the other person, needing their approval or validation, or having difficulty making decisions without their input.

Inability to Move Forward:

Feeling stuck in a past relationship or pattern, unable to move on or find new connections.

Jealousy or Possessiveness:

Experiencing intense feelings of jealousy or possessiveness towards the other person, or difficulty trusting them.

Feeling of Being Controlled:

Feeling that the other person is controlling or manipulating your thoughts, emotions, or behavior.

Intense Spiritual connection:

Feeling your souls are united as one, and that the "tie" is binding you to a person you do not want to be bound to, and is hampering your efforts at moving forward in life.

Persistent Feelings of Shame and Unworthiness:

Feeling depressed, shame, feeling you are not being good enough, or unworthy of affection.

Sinful Actions:

Engaging in actions that are harmful to yourself or others, such as infidelity, addiction, or abuse.

Unexplained Emotional Turmoil:

Feeling an emotional connection that causes pain or suffering.

How and Why Do You Need to Break Soul Ties?

Soul ties can hinder spiritual growth and create unhealthy dependencies, as it is particularly built on sin, unhealthy attachment, or a lack of boundaries that can lead to emotional, spiritual, or even physical harm. While the term "soul tie" is not explicitly used in the Bible, the concept is clearly present.

"Do you not know that he who unites himself with a prostitute is one with her in body? For it is said, 'The two will become one flesh.' But whoever is united with the Lord is one with him in spirit." *1 Corinthians 6:16-17.*

This passage highlights the spiritual impact of sexual unions and the importance of being united with the Lord instead of ungodly connections. Christ has "canceled the charge of our legal indebtedness, which stood against us and condemned us; He has taken it away, nailing it to the cross." *Colossians 2:14.*

It is through Christ, you have the power to be free from spiritual bondages, including Soul Ties, by doing the following.

Acknowledge the Need:

Begin by honestly acknowledging the need for breaking the Soul Tie and the hurt it has caused.

Seek Repentance, Forgiveness, and Healing:

Repent of anything you did to participate in the Soul Tie. Ask God for forgiveness for any part you played in the relationship and for healing from any emotional wounds.

Renounce Unhealthy Agreements:

Explicitly renounce any vows, agreements, or commitments that are not in line with God's will.

Request for the Soul Tie to Be Broken:

Ask God to break any unholy bonds and sever any connections that are not pleasing to Him.

Surrender to God:

Express your desire to surrender your heart and life to God's guidance and love.

Pray in Faith:

Pray with faith, believing that God can break the soul tie and restore you to wholeness.

Personalize Your Prayer:

Tailor the prayer to your specific situation and needs, using your own words and expressing your heart to God.

Breaking Soul Ties Through Prayer

"Lord, I ask for your guidance and strength, so that all unhealthy Soul Ties can be broken. I acknowledge that I have been hurt, and I repent that I have hurt others. I ask for your forgiveness and healing. I renounce any unholy agreements or vows that I may have made, and I ask that you sever any connections that are not pleasing to You. Amen"

For each person you can think of, say out loud with their name inserted. Keep going until you cannot remember anyone else. If you remember someone later, pause and repeat the phrase below.

In the name of Jesus Christ, I break every soul tie and every unholy bond with _____.

I give back what I took from _____ and I take back what I gave _____.

"I surrender my heart to you Lord, and I ask that you fill me with your love and peace. In Your Holy name, Amen".

What Are Generational Curses?

Generational Curses can produce misfortune, negative traits, and negative behaviors, especially dysfunctional behaviors. They are often rooted in sin or trauma. Generational Curses are passed from one generation to the next.

The experiences of your ancestors can create a negative legacy and impact subsequent generations. Until these Generational Curses are broken, this can lead to your future family members repeating the sins and negative patterns of their ancestors. "You shall not bow down to them nor serve them. For I, the Lord your God, am a jealous God, visiting the iniquity of the fathers upon the children to the third and fourth generations of those who hate Me, but showing mercy to thousands, to those who love Me and keep My commandments." *Exodus 20:5-6.* "The Lord is slow to anger and abounding in steadfast love, forgiving iniquity and to the third and the fourth generation." *Hebrews 14:18.*

Why Break Generational Cures?

Breaking generational curses is making the conscious decision to stop practicing, absorbing, and passing on toxic behaviors and personality traits to your children and future generations. Some of these toxic personality traits can be anger, violence, manipulation, lying, being overly critical, lying, cheating, stealing, and addiction, to name a few. Sin can be passed from generation to generation. This is particularly true of addictive behaviors such as alcoholism, drugs, and sex. Similarly, physical and sexual abuse might become ingrained in the legacy for certain families. Deliverance from these curses is available to everyone who sincerely calls upon the name of Jesus.

"Therefore there is now no condemnation for those who are in Christ Jesus." *Romans 8:1.*

"everyone who calls on the name of the Lord will be saved." *Romans 10:13.* Jesus, however, challenges this idea of inherited guilt.

"And do not be conformed to this world, but be transformed by the renewal of your mind, that by testing you may discern what is the will of God, what is acceptable and perfect." *Romans 12:1-2*.

When his disciples asked if a blind man was born blind because of his own sins or his parents' sins, Jesus responded, "Neither this man nor his parents sinned, but this happened so that the works of God might be displayed in his life." *John 9:2-3*.

How to Break Generational Curses

While the Bible acknowledges the impact of past sins, it also emphasizes the importance of repentance, forgiveness, and seeking God's grace to overcome generational patterns of sin. If you are living under a generational curse, it will be cancelled when you repent with faith and renounce the curse.

A Prayer to Repent and Break Off Generational Curses

Say this prayer for one person at a time and continue until you cannot remember any more names. If you should remember another name, stop and repeat the prayer. If you are unable to remember the name, just say that person.

Father,

I repent of my sins and those of _____ (name)

I break every oath, every vow, pledge and ceremony. I renounce it under the blood of Jesus.

I thank you, God, that generational curses are broken through faith in the Lord Jesus. I believe Jesus is my strength and that His blood cancels any curse and breaks any generational sins. I believe that any generational curse is cancelled and broken off my family now, in Jesus' name. Thank you that sins, bondages, and iniquities are cancelled and any curse is stopped by the blood of Jesus. Thank you that through Jesus, no curse will be passed to another generation. Amen.

What Is Spiritual Trauma?

Spiritual trauma refers to the impact of traumatic events on your sense of meaning, self-concept, and relationship with your faith in God. In some cases, it can involve changes in belief systems, questioning your faith, or feeling abandoned by God. Spiritual abuse is demonic and a form of emotional manipulation that can also worsen your trauma, using religious beliefs or authority structures to justify abusive behavior. A traumatic event can cause you to experience changes in the way you see God, such as feeling abandoned or punished by Him, feeling angry at Him, or questioning how the loving, all-powerful God could allow horrible things to happen to the innocent. All of which are demonic thoughts.

Your spiritual life helps build a closer relationship with God. This close relationship to God buffers the effects of a trauma and provides a source of comfort during times of distress. This relationship can happen because you can increase your faith after a traumatic event, as your relationship with God becomes even more meaningful to you. When this happens, you find a greater sense of purpose in life and a new closeness to God: you see the ability to work with God to solve problems, relieve pain, and give forgiveness.

To achieve all of this, forgiving yourself and others is the way God planned it. Jesus emphasizes the importance of forgiveness, both from God and from others. His teachings highlight forgiveness as a core principle for believers. Urging you to forgive others as you have been forgiven by God. Forgiveness is a key to your relationship with others and with Him. This is shown clearly in the Lord's Prayer, where Jesus teaches, "Forgive us our debts, as we also have forgiven our debtors." *Matthew 6:12.*

A traumatic event can cause you to experience changes in the way you see God, such as feelings of being abandoned or punished by Him, feeling angry at Him because He did not step in and stop the abuse, or questioning how a loving, all-powerful God can allow horrible things to happen to the innocent. When you struggle to make sense of a trauma, your belief in God may falter, and unforgiveness then takes hold. All of this opens the door for demons to step right in. Demons can cause you to feel there is no God, or God does not care, or God does not love you. If God cared, this would have never happened. Where was Jesus? With the experience of this type of traumatic event, you can think that this is punishment from God. You feel that the world is more cruel than you previously thought. God is not that good, Jesus really does not care, and the Holy Spirit does not exist. This causes more spiritual injury and guilt, as well as difficulties with forgiveness. Demons rejoice because there is a victim they can control and influence as they entice you to see life as negative or evil. But, more importantly to demons, there is no God. Without repentance and turning back to God, they just stole a soul from God.

All of this opens doors for demons to influence or control your life. Not only your spiritual life, but also your relationship with God. There is less, if any, forgiveness given. There is less relationship with God, and there is less prayer life. There is less reading of the Bible for direction. There is less reliance on God for anything. And, the worst for you is to think there is no God, and you walk away from Him. So things get much worse due to this trauma, and the demons who take over the mind, body, and emotions are delighted. Of course, this can also lead to mental illness or suicide.

What To Do?

For serenity, you need to face the trauma with God holding you up. He is good and has already defeated Satan and all demons. There is hope not only now, but in the future. He loves you more than you can imagine. He is listening to you, cares for you, and guides you. God is good. He holds you in the palm of His hand. He is there with you always, even in the worst of times. Even though it does not seem God is there at all, God holds you up, comforts, and protects you, no matter the circumstances.

Psalm 91 is a powerful declaration of faith and trust in God's protection and provision. It emphasizes God's love and care for those who love Him, offering assurances of security and deliverance in times of trouble. The psalmist speaks of God as a refuge and a fortress, promising to shield and protect those who dwell in His presence. It is important to trust God's power, the power that created the Universe. We need to trust in that same power and seek His presence.

His outstretched arms are waiting for you to take refuge in Him and to trust in His ability to protect and guide you as He is constantly involved in your life, constantly there. He cares and brings comfort to you in times of need, even if you do not recognize it immediately. He does not turn away from you. God provides you with strength and comfort even when you face terrible hardships. He never leaves you, even if you do not feel His presence. He is always there with hope and assurance, and you are never alone. All you have to do is turn your face towards Him and know that He is the God of love, compassion, understanding, patience, and strength to carry you when you need Him to.

"Whoever dwells in the shelter of the Most High will rest in the shadow of the Almighty, I will say of the Lord, He is my refuge and my fortress, my God, in whom I trust." Surely he will save you from the fowler's snare and the deadly pestilence. He will cover you with his feathers, and under his wings you will find refuge; his faithfulness will be your shield and rampart. You will not fear the terror of night, nor the arrow that flies by day, nor the pestilence that stalks in the darkness, nor the plague that destroys at midday. A thousand may fall at your side, ten thousand at your right hand, but it will not come near you. You will only observe with your eyes and see the punishment of the wicked. If you say, "The Lord is my refuge," and you make the Most High your dwelling, no harm will overtake you, no disaster will come near your tent. For he will command his angels concerning you to guard you in all your ways; they will lift you up in their hands, so that you will not strike your foot against a stone. You will tread on the lion and the cobra; you will trample the great lion and the serpent. "Because he loves me," says the Lord, "I will rescue him; I will protect him, for he acknowledges my name. He will call on me, and I will answer him; I will be with him in trouble, I will deliver him and honor him. With long life, I will satisfy him and show him my salvation."

How Do You Bind Demons?

The word "bind" means to tie or fasten something tightly. Binding a demon is the act of restricting or restraining a demon's activity, influence, or control. Binding is usually not permanent. It is often done through prayer and is considered a way to bring evil forces into submission.

Jesus dealt with the demonic realm a great deal in the gospels, primarily in the context of casting them out. He opened the way for the disciples to cast out demons also. The disciples cast out demons and taught other believers to do the same. It is said that driving out demons was one of the signs to fellow believers.

Jesus gives a teaching to His disciples on binding and loosing. Jesus gave the apostles sole authority to bind and loose things on earth. Jesus says, "You are Peter, and upon this rock I will build My church; and the gates of Hades shall not overpower it. I will give you the keys of the kingdom of heaven; and whatever you shall bind on earth shall be bound in heaven, and whatever you shall loose on earth shall be loosed in heaven." In *Matthew 16:18-19*.

"And I saw an angel coming down out of heaven, having the key to the Abyss and holding in his hand a great chain. He seized the dragon, that ancient serpent, which is the devil or Satan, and bound him for a thousand years." An angel binds Satan for a thousand years, so there is a precedent. *Revelation 20:2*.

Mark 3:27 and *Matthew 12:29* tell us that before we can enter a strong man's (Satan's) house unless we must first bind him. By any reasonable measure, that scripture applies to demons.

Believers have been given authority over demons. There can be positive benefits from binding demons. It is best not to take on Binding Satan himself. In the context of demonic oppression, it is appropriate for you to bind tormenting demons who are at work in a person's life.

Bound Demon

This is a critical clarification: a bound demon is not the same as Deliverance. A bound demon can be loosed by a person's free will. Binding effectively lasts only as long as it lasts! The duration can be minutes, hours, days, weeks, or more. A person's free will determines how long the demon will stay bound. By their free will, the Demons will be loosed again. In other words, Binding is not permanent. The binding can be repeated by you if needed.

What is Binding and Loosing

The Binding of a demon can make it become inactive, so that the Holy Spirit can minister to the person being affected and to those people negatively affected by that person. As you pray for loved ones, families, friends, and ministries, some will have positive results, some will not. When you engage in binding, you are recognizing and proactively declaring that the struggle is not against flesh and blood, but against demons. *Ephesians 5:12*.

How To Bind Demons

Binding a demon can be done through prayer. As a believer, you have been given authority over demonic spirits. Binding is appropriate for demons at work in a person's life. It does not need to be done in front of the person; in fact, that can inflame the demons even more. Demons are bound by Jesus Christ when we ask Him.

Binding a Demon Through Prayer

Say Out Loud

"In the name of Jesus Christ, I bind up that spirit of _____ with the blood of Jesus. You will not be active, you will not communicate with or draw strength from any other spirits. In the name of Jesus Christ, you will not harm or torment _____."

(Name the demon if you know it, or how the demon is affecting the person's life. Such as anger, stress, depression, immorality, etc.)

"Holy Spirit, I ask you to reveal God's great love for (Name) _____. Holy Spirit, please provide help and healing to _____ and a full acceptance of God's Love and Guidance. Let godly actions and. desires be consistently shown in _____ in service to You."

Prayer of Gratitude

"Heavenly Father, I thank you, God, for your love, care, and protection during this time. I praise you for binding the demons that are oppressing_____. I ask for your protection, guidance, and the empowerment of your Holy Spirit by _____. Please fill _____ - with your light, strength, and wisdom. Help _____ to resist any further demonic influence.

In the name of Jesus, I renounce all demonic activity and renounce any negative vows or curses that have formed against _____. I pray for forgiveness for any sins _____ has committed. I commit myself to help _____ to live a life that is pleasing to you. Amen"

Spiritual Warfare Scriptures

The concept of "God reading the word" refers to the idea that God's Word, often understood as the Bible, is a living and active force, a source of divine truth and guidance, and a reflection of God's character and will.

"Submit yourselves to God. Resist the devil, and he will flee from you." *James 4:7.*

"You are from God, little children, and have overcome them; because greater is He who is in you than he who is in the world." *1 John 4:4.*

"For though we live in the world, we do not wage war as the world does. The weapons we fight with are not the weapons of the world. On the contrary, they have divine power to demolish strongholds. We demolish arguments and every pretension that sets itself up against the knowledge of God, and we take captive every thought to make it obedient to Christ." *2 Corinthians 10:3-5.*

"Be self-controlled and alert. Your enemy, the devil prowls around like a roaring lion looking for someone to devour. Resist him, standing firm in the faith." *1 Peter. 5:8-9.*

"No weapon that is formed against you will prosper; and every tongue that accuses you in judgment you will condemn. This is the heritage of the servants of the Lord, and their vindication is from Me," declares the Lord." *Isaiah 54:17.*

"Put on the full armor of God, so that you can take your stand against the devil's schemes. For our struggle is not against flesh and blood, but against the rulers, against the authorities, against the powers of this dark world and against the spiritual forces of evil in the heavenly realms. Therefore, put on the full armor of God, so that when the day of evil comes, you may be able to stand your ground, and after you have done everything, to stand. Stand firm then, with the belt of truth buckled around your waist, with the breastplate of righteousness in place, and with your feet fitted with the readiness that comes from the gospel of peace. In addition to all this, take up the shield of faith, with which you can extinguish all the flaming arrows of the evil one. Take the helmet of salvation and the sword of the Spirit, which is the word of God." *Ephesians 6:11-1.*

"In all these things, we are more than conquerors through Him who loved us." *Romans. 8:37.*

"But thanks be to God, who gives us the victory through our Lord Jesus Christ." *1 Corinthians 15:57.*

"Not by might nor by power, but by My Spirit,' says the Lord of hosts." *Zechariah. 4:6.*

"But the Lord is faithful, and he will strengthen you and protect you from the evil one." *2 Thessalonians 3:3.*

"Behold, I have given you authority to tread on serpents and scorpions, and over all the power of the enemy, and nothing shall hurt you." *Luke 10:19.*

"The thief comes only to steal and kill and destroy. I came that they may have life and have it abundantly." *John 10:10.*

"Truly I tell you, whatever you bind on earth will be bound in heaven, and whatever you loose on earth will be loosed in heaven. Again, truly I tell you that if two of you on earth agree about anything they ask for, it will be done for them by my Father in heaven." *Matthew 18:18-19.*

"The Lord will cause your enemies who rise against you to be defeated before you. They shall come out against you one way and flee before you seven ways." *Deuteronomy 28:7.*

"I have told you these things, so that in me you may have peace. In this world you will have trouble. But take heart! I have overcome the world." *John 16:33.*

"No temptation has overtaken you except what is common to mankind. And God is faithful; he will not let you be tempted beyond what you can bear. But when you are tempted, he will also provide a way out so that you can endure it." *1 Corinthians 10:13.*

"And you will know the truth, and the truth will set you free." *John 8:32.*

"Do not be overcome with evil, but overcome evil with good." *Romans 12:21.*

"And they have conquered him by the blood of the Lamb and by the word of their testimony, for hey loved not their lives even unto death." *Revelations 12:11.*

"Fight the good fight of the faith. Take hold of the eternal life to which you were called when you made your good confession in the presence of many witnesses." *1 Timothy. 6:12.*

"On this rock I will build my church, and the gates of hell shall not prevail against it." *Matthew 16:8.*

"…the reason the Son of God appeared was to destroy the devil's work." *1 John 3:8.*

"But they who wait for the Lord shall renew their strength; they shall mount up with wings like eagles; they shall run and not be weary; they shall walk and not faint." *Isaiah 40:31.*

"One of your men puts to flight a thousand, for the Lord your God is He who fights for you, just as He promised you." *Joshua. 23:10.*

"Do not fear them, for the Lord your God is the one fighting for you." *Deuteronomy 3:22.*

"What then shall we say to these things? If God is for us, who is against us?" *Romans. 8:31.*

"Through You we will push back our adversaries, through Your name we will trample down those who rise up against us." *Psalm. 44:5.*

"Have I not commanded you? Be strong and courageous! Do not tremble or be dismayed, for the Lord your God is with you wherever you go." *Joshua. 1:9.*

"For You have girded me with strength for battle; You have subdued under me those who rose up against me." *Psalm 18:39.*

"He who dwells in the shelter of the Most High will rest in the shadow of the Almighty. I will say of the Lord, He is my refuge and my fortress, my

God, in whom I trust. Surely, he will save you under his wings you will find refuge; his faithfulness will be your shield and rampart..." *Psalms 91:1-4.*

"This is what the Lord says to you: 'Do not be afraid or discouraged because of this vast army. For the battle is not yours, but God's." *2 Chronicles. 20:15.*

The battle belongs to the Lord, and He has the final victory!

EPILOGUE

Your Ongoing Battle and Your Responsibility to Protect Your Children

Throughout this journey, you have confronted the dark forces of Satan and learned how to shield yourself from his power and the schemes of his demons. You have fought spiritual battles, guarding your heart and mind through faith, prayer, and the strength that comes from Jesus Christ. But your personal battle does not end with you; it grows even more urgent when it comes to protecting the most vulnerable among you: your children.

Satan knows that children are his easiest targets. From infancy, he seeks to infiltrate their minds and hearts, sway their choices, and shape their futures according to his will. The young are the foundation of tomorrow, and if you leave them unguarded, their lives can slowly fall under his control, setting them on a path far from God's love and protection.

As a parent, guardian, or caretaker, you bear a new responsibility in this spiritual battleground. What can you do to keep your child safe from these dark influences? How can you teach them, guard them, and nurture their faith so that evil finds no foothold?

The Bible gives you powerful wisdom and reassurance about this challenge. Jesus Christ himself emphasized the sacred place of children in God's kingdom, urging you to guide them as you protect their innocence and faith. In His words, "Let the little children come to me, and do not hinder them, for the kingdom of heaven belongs to such as these." *(Matthew 19:14)* This divine call reminds you that children are precious and that their spiritual well-being must be fiercely guarded.

That is why "How to Beat Satan and Free Your Family, A Parent's Guide for Spiritual Warfare" is more than just a book, it is a vital tool for every parent determined to defend their children against the enemy's tactics. It will give you practical guidance, biblical truths, and a clear path to reclaim your family's spiritual freedom.

Make this next book your priority. The fight your children face today is serious and real, and the knowledge and strategies you will gain are essential for safeguarding their hearts and souls from demonic oppression. Together, with the power of Jesus, the guidance of the Holy Spirit, and the love of God, you can protect their future and lead your family into the light.

www.ingramcontent.com/pod-product-compliance
Lightning Source LLC
Chambersburg PA
CBHW061801070526
44586CB00023B/2659